FUNDAMENTALISM:

HAZARDS AND HEARTBREAKS

Fundamentalism:

HAZARDS AND HEARTBREAKS

Rod L. Evans

AND

Irwin M. Berent

Foreword by Steve Allen

Introduction by Isaac Asimov

Open  Court

La Salle, Illinois 61301

✼

OPEN COURT and the above logo are registered in the U.S. Patent and Trademark Office.

First printing 1988
Second printing 1990

Printed and bound in the United States of America.

Library of Congress Cataloging-in-Publication Data

Evans, Rod L., 1956-
    Fundamentalism : hazards and heartbreaks / Rod L. Evans and Irwin
M. Berent ; foreword by Steve Allen ; introduction by Isaac Asimov.
        p.   cm.
    Bibliography: p.
    Includes index.
    ISBN 0-8126-9080-X : $26.95.   ISBN 0-8126-9081-8 (pbk.) : $11.95
        1. Fundamentalism—Controversial literature.   2. Bible-
-Inspiration—Controverisal literature.   I. Berent, Irwin M.
    II. Title.
    BT82.2.E92   1988
    280'.4—dc19

#18222719   88-21885
                                                                                              CIP

ACKNOWLEDGMENTS

We wish to express our gratitude to Dr. William Brenner, philosophy professor, the Reverend R. Lee Carter, Baptist minister, Dr. Frederick M. Denny, professor of religion, David Ramsay Steele, our editor, and, of course, both Isaac Asimov and Steve Allen. We deeply appreciate the insightful advice given to us by Dr. Brenner, the Reverend Carter, and Dr. Denny. We are especially thankful to Mr. Steele for his copious and perceptive suggestions. Naturally, we feel honored that Isaac Asimov has been so gracious as to take time to write our introduction, and that Steve Allen thought so highly of our work that he contributed the foreword. Although we have profited from the advice given to us, we, of course, take responsibility for all views expressed by us in the book.

ROD L. EVANS
IRWIN M. BERENT

Contents

Foreword

Those who preach sweet reason will never have an easy time of it in a largely irrational world. In recent centuries it was assumed that by the time man reached the present period of history superstition and religious fanaticism, among other unedifying weaknesses, would have been largely supplanted by an 'age of reason', but by no means necessarily one in which either atheism or agnosticism were the norm.

It is now all too painfully obvious that rosy predictions about the almost inevitable progressive development of social sanity were very wide of the mark. Indeed the amount of rabid and unreasonable behavior, within religious, political and nationalist contexts, would appear to be as tragically bad as ever. But such uncomfortable facts can never be marshalled to construct an argument for apathy or resignation. There is more need than ever for appealing to an ideal in which reason and faith can be experienced in a harmonious rather than antagonistic relationship. It is, in any event, clear that those believers who reject reason are doing enormous harm to their own cause, for if there are millions who know little and care less about the necessity of the search for truth that respects clear evidence, there are other millions who will simply turn their backs on religious belief if the examples of it they encounter are characterized by a closed-mindedness that starts with a conclusion and simply tosses overboard or distorts any evidence that appears to call into question the original assumption. Evans and Berent have done a superb job of considering the fundamentalist mind-set in a fair, reasonable way. This book deserves the most careful scrutiny by both fundamentalists and those who do not share their approach to the worship of God.

STEVE ALLEN

INTRODUCTION

I am a member of 'The Baker Street Irregulars'. We are a band of enthusiasts devoted to the sixty Sherlock Holmes stories, which some of us refer to as the 'canon' and some as 'the sacred writings'.

It is customary among us to suppose that the stories are true tales that tell of actual events. We suppose that Dr. John H. Watson is the real narrator of all the stories but two, and that he and Sherlock Holmes are real people. In fact, there is a certain reluctance among us of the BSI to admit that either is actually dead even now. We tend to envisage them as living in quiet retirement, even though Sherlock Holmes must now be 132 years old.

As for Sir Arthur Conan Doyle—well, he was only Watson's agent.

A further axiom concerning the Sherlock Holmes stories is that they are 'inerrant', that they contain no mistakes or contradictions. This gives us plenty of opportunity for 're-search' and for the preparation of 'learned papers'.

From casual references in a particular story to the state of the weather, or the arrival of the mail, the date on which a particular adventure took place may be reasoned out. From other references, numerous other conclusions may be drawn—where Holmes had spent his time during years in which he was lost track of, how many wives Watson had had, whether Holmes went to Oxford or Cambridge, and so on.

Now the fact is that Conan Doyle grew heartily sick of Sherlock Holmes after a while. The extraordinary popularity of the character drowned out the other books he was writing and he himself was lost in the blaze of Sherlock Holmes. He tried to stop writing the stories, he tried to raise his price, he even tried to kill Holmes. Nothing helped. He became the highest paid writer in the world—provided he would continue to write Holmes stories. So he did, as quickly and as angrily as possible.

The result is that he did not much care what he wrote and he managed to introduce many inconsistencies and errors. Nevertheless, by the doctrine of 'inerrancy' all must be explained and *are*. The ingenuity of the BSI members can meet the challenge. Thus, in one of the stories, Mrs. John H. Watson refers to her husband as "James". Clearly this is one of Conan Doyle's careless mistakes that was not caught by a proofreader. However, a learned paper pointed out that the middle initial H. might well stand for 'Hamish', which is a Scottish equivalent of James and reams of reasoning were brought out to support this hypothesis—and the result was roundly applauded as a gem of Sherlockian research.

The important thing to remember, however, is that this is a game! No two members of the BSI interpret a particular item in the same way, but we have no heresies, no hard feelings, no arguments, no denunciations, no excommunications. In fact, if any BSI member were to imply that in cold reality, he believed that Sherlock Holmes was alive, that the stories were all true, and that Watson's middle name was Hamish, we would all seriously suspect his sanity.

But there *is* a sacred book in our culture, and many *do* consider it inerrant. It is the Bible. The Bible consists of many parts written by many people. Some of the prophetic books were written as early as the 8th Century B.C., some others were written later but contain legendary material dating back to the Sumerians; say, to 2000 B.C. On the other hand, the Book of Revelation may have been written in A.D. 90.

It is not surprising if material written by many people over many centuries should contradict itself here and there; or if much of what it says is not consonant with modern scientific knowledge.

However, to those who believe in the inerrancy of the Bible, it was written by God and the men who *seemed* to write it were under the influence of divine inspiration and were merely God's scribes. If there are apparent errors or inconsistencies, those are only apparent and can be explained away and for a couple of thousand years very brilliant men have worked at the necessary interpretations.

And they have succeeded, too. Everything has been interpreted, everything has been made clear. The only trouble is that no two interpreters end up with quite the same interpretation. And since the Bible is much more important than Sherlock Holmes, and the interpreters of the former much more serious than those of the latter, the differences in interpretation have led to heresies, hard feelings, arguments, denunciations, excommunications and worse: torture, death by fire, to say nothing of long and bitter wars in which armies, all of whom accepted the sacredness of the Bible, inflicted atrocities on each other and on the surrounding population because interpretations differed.

In this book you hold, whose entire aura is one of reason and peaceful persuasion, the Bible is treated as though it meant what it said, and said what it meant, and its contradictions are pointed out. It makes the Bible no less sacred and no less useful if we consider it a human book and don't play foolish intellectual games with it that lead to hatred, death, and destruction.

ISAAC ASIMOV

PREFACE

$\mathbf{W}$e hope that fundamentalists and non-fundamentalists alike will find this a useful book that helps them more clearly to understand and appreciate themselves and one another. Some people who have adopted Christian fundamentalism are experiencing feelings of doubt, frustration, even anguish. This book seeks to present a reliable diagnosis of what are the probable causes of that pain. We do not claim to have all the answers to this question. There are, indeed, many *possible* explanations: Perhaps some fundamentalists are taking up fundamentalism for unhealthy reasons. Or perhaps they are bringing to their fundamentalist experiences certain negative psychological traits. Perhaps they are somehow misreading the Bible, or maybe they are over-using the Bible (if, indeed, that is possible to do with such a magnificent work). Or perhaps there are other reasons for their distress?

One thing, however, is clear: If the fundamentalists' problems relate in *any* way to their approaches to the Bible, everyone should be concerned. For whatever may be one's feelings about the Bible, that awesome document is undeniably both too significant for people to want it neglected and too powerful for people to want it misused.

THE BIBLE

Many people respond to the Bible with either uncritical allegiance or total rejection. Both responses lead to a reduced appreciation of the Bible's value and often result from misconceptions about the way in which the Bible was written and transmitted. Scholars have studied the Bible more extensively than perhaps any other book, yet the average person's response to it is often naive. Many people reject the

Bible without sympathetic study, while many others believe that it is a book without error, nowhere reflecting human imperfection.

Most believers in the perfection of the Bible maintain that respect for the Bible requires the belief that it is inerrant, that is, free from error of every sort. Holding that belief, most but not all people who call themselves 'fundamentalists' often view the Bible as representing the very Word of God, dictated to writers who were Divinely preserved from error. The truth of Christianity becomes dependent on the inerrancy of the Bible, which is regarded as something resembling a seamless web whose integrity is seriously threatened by the least rupture. Doubts about the truth of any Biblical claim are seen as immoral if not Satanic.

THE PURPOSE OF THIS BOOK

This book is written not to discourage either faith in God or reverence for the Bible, but rather to point out some potential hazards associated with viewing the Bible in the ways in which many fundamentalists typically view it. In so doing, it is hoped that readers of this book will not only more fully understand fundamentalism, but also more fully understand themselves, the Bible, and their religious beliefs. This book will be especially helpful to those who have become converted to fundamentalism and then been faced by frightening doubts or those who have abandoned fundamentalism to adjust. And in its attempt to explain reasons for the difficulties often associated with holding belief in the doctrine of Biblical inerrancy, this book will be enlightening to those who are simply curious about fundamentalism.

We, the authors, are not motivated by animosity toward fundamentalists. We are not 'secular humanists', nor are we 'fanatical liberals'. We believe in God and love the Bible. Our chief purpose in writing this book is to further the pursuit of truth, a quest to which both fundamentalists and non-fundamentalists can easily relate. We believe that God created the human brain to be used honestly and sincerely in the pursuit of truth, not uncritically in promotion of dogma. When we discuss 'fundamentalists' and 'fundamentalism', our intent is not to overgeneralize about a group of people or their beliefs. We sincerely mean no disrespect. 'Fundamentalists' are *not*, in real life, a monolithic group, sharing identical beliefs. When we use the term 'fundamentalist', *our primary focus is on the majority of fundamentalists, who believe that the Bible is infallible.*

We maintain that, in general, the greater the degree to which fundamentalists unquestioningly accept the doctrine of Biblical inerrancy, the greater the risk to their fullest understanding and appreciation of the Bible. By treating the Bible as inerrant, fundamentalists may become increasingly unable to conceive how human limitations in wisdom and knowledge could have influenced the Bible. And the most devout fundamentalists may find great difficulty in appreciating the degree to which historical conditions have also influenced it. Whenever they come upon even the least inconsistency in the Bible, they may be unable to acknowledge it with a historically sensitive awareness. Yet this rigid belief in inerrancy requires them somehow to dissolve any such 'errors' to retain their faith. In contrast, many non-fundamentalists can easily adapt their faith to a scientific appreciation of virtually any implausibility, inconsistency, or cultural bias that may appear in the Bible.

This book is intended to serve as an easy-to-read guide to understanding some of the most serious risks to which fundamentalists expose themselves. The book is organized as follows. Chapter 1 provides a brief definition of 'fundamentalism' and 'fundamentalists'. Chapter 2 examines the claims of former fundamentalists who believe that the methods of the religious instruction to which they were exposed have caused them psychological trauma. Chapter 3 discusses the impact of some teachings of two leading conservative evangelists, Pat Robertson and Jerry Falwell. Chapter 4 attempts to explain why some people are attracted to fundamentalist approaches to the Bible, while others believe that those approaches tend to be wooden and narrow, and prefer to look at the Bible in other ways.

Chapters 5 through 10 point out particular implausibilities or inconsistencies that many fundamentalists, because of their belief in the doctrine of Biblical inerrancy, often may be unable to recognize. Chapter 5 presents examples of incredible Biblical narratives, pointing out the need for appreciating the pre-scientific views of the Biblical writers. That chapter also includes a discussion of the theory of evolution and cites some of the views of Pat Robertson to illustrate how some people have tried to use the Bible to oppose modern science. Chapter 6 describes the ways in which the Biblical writers tended to ascribe to God their sometimes dubious points of view. That chapter also makes a case for Biblical moral progress. Chapter 7 presents some considerations necessary for achieving a balanced view of the Biblical Jesus. Chapter 8 points out popular misconceptions about the Bible. Chapter 9 discusses how some people used Scripture to justify intolerance. And Chapter 10 describes the ways in which some New Testament writers controversially used Old Testament Scripture.

Chapter 11 points out many of the historical conditions that most likely influenced the writing of the Bible. That chapter, along with Chapter 12, offers some sensitive, practical measures that can be taken to avoid some of the most serious hazards associated with Christian fundamentalism.

Any information about the Bible discussed in this book is probably quite familiar to most if not all Biblical scholars. Although it is not intended to introduce those scholars to new research, it is hoped that, by exposing laypersons to modern Biblical scholarship, the book will also contribute, in some modest way, to bridging the gap in knowledge between laypersons and scholars. We have researched this book thoroughly, and it has been checked throughout by scholarly experts, to ensure that it contains no mistakes. But this work is not primarily addressed to scholars, and it doesn't pretend to give a full account of fundamentalism. It is a practical approach to problems, and is addressed to the general reader or ordinary churchgoer. For such a reader, we hope this book may be an introduction to wider study. In 'What to Read Next', at the end of the book, we give suggestions for further reading.

Parts of the book seek to bring together many of the ideas about Biblical scholarship otherwise contained in an enormous array of literature. Much of that literature is often not easily accessible or easily understandable to the average layperson; some of it is even insensitive and sarcastic. This book instead employs a non-inflammatory approach to an issue that has all too often divided people into emotional factions and driven them to maintain positions not fully sensitive to opposing viewpoints. It is hoped that a calm approach will stimulate thoughtful discussion rather than promote discord.

A NOTE ON BIBLICAL REFERENCES

Most Bible verses quoted herein are taken from *The Book* (Wheaton, Ill.: Tyndale House, 1984), which is *The Living Bible* (Wheaton Ill.: Tyndale House, 1971) in paragraph form. *The Book* was chosen for two reasons. First, it is a highly readable paraphrase in everyday language. Second, *The Book* has been widely promoted, especially by the Christian Broadcasting Network (C.B.N.), which was headed by M. G. 'Pat' Robertson. Many, though certainly not all, fundamentalists have regarded *The Book*, Mr. Robertson, and C.B.N. as representing their points of view in Biblical matters.

We do not pretend that *The Book* is the most accurate representation of the Bible. Since *The Book* is a paraphrase, we made sure that the verses cited are substantially similar in meaning to the corresponding verses in such established translations as the *King James Version* and *Revised Standard Version*. We are alert to the differences in meaning among different versions and paraphrases. Indeed, we have devoted a section of our book to describing some ways in which different representations of the Bible can reflect the preferred interpretations of those who translate or paraphrase the Bible.

Where the beliefs or attitudes of "Matthew", "Mark", "Luke", or "John" are mentioned or discussed, no theory of authorship is implied.

CHAPTER 1

WHAT IS FUNDAMENTALISM? WHO ARE

FUNDAMENTALISTS?

Before one can begin to become aware of any potential hazards in Christian fundamentalism, it is helpful first to understand both what Christian fundamentalism *is* and who 'Christian fundamentalists' *are*. It is, indeed, possible that, in at least some respects, some people are fundamentalists and do not even know it.

The term 'fundamentalist' originally referred to Christians who followed tenets, or 'fundamentals', of Christian faith as laid down principally in a publication of volumes widely circulated between 1910 and 1915, entitled *The Fundamentals*. Fundamentalism was a reaction against the movement of twentieth-century modernism, whose Biblical criticism, religious liberalism, rationalism, geology, astronomy, and theory of evolution were perceived as opponents of true Christianity. (The label 'fundamentalism' has subsequently been applied to movements within other religions, such as Hinduism or Islam. In this book we are concerned only with Christian fundamentalism.)

Many avowed fundamentalists today still adhere to most of those original fundamentals, and remain opposed to much of modern science and Liberal Christianity, preferring to separate themselves from what they consider an essentially evil world. Yet fundamentalism today is more an ideology than a movement, and most of its adherents are not so easily defined. People who adhere to at least some of the principles of fundamentalism can be found in almost any Christian denomination, but fundamentalism itself is not a denomination. Further, while there are some non-denominational, or independent, churches that are considered 'fundamentalist churches', people who consider themselves 'fundamentalist' may be a small percentage of the actual number of people who hold fundamentalist beliefs. Still further, the 'electronic' churches of such televangelists as Jerry Falwell, Jimmy Swaggart, Oral Roberts, and Ernest Angley are often heavily fundamentalist in orientation; yet many of their viewers may in fact not have a clearly defined notion of what kinds of beliefs are being communicated.

The 'fundamentals of the faith' that are held by the avowed 'fundamentalists', as well as by any people who generally hold fundamentalist beliefs, vary somewhat from group to group. Those fundamentals usually include beliefs that Jesus Christ is God, that he was born of a virgin, that he died for all sin as God's substitute for man ('substitutionary' or 'vicarious atonement'), that he rose bodily from the dead ('literal resurrection'), and that he will return in bodily form ('Second Coming'). Other beliefs often include belief in the existence of the Father, Son, and Holy Ghost (Trinity or 'Triune God'), in the reality of Satan, in eternal bliss and punishment, in original sin, in salvation through grace rather than through good works, and in the approaching thousand-year earthly reign of Jesus ('pre-millenialism'). In addition, soul-winning, Divine healing, being 'born again' or spiritually transformed, being baptized by immersion, speaking in tongues, living a life of holiness and separation from the world, are practices and beliefs common to some but by no means all fundamentalist groups. Of course, one does not have to be a fundamentalist to hold many, if not most, of those beliefs.

The fundamentalist also believes that the final authority for any tenet of the faith must firmly rest with the Bible. If fundamentalists did not believe this primary tenet, that the entire Bible represents God's communication with man ('inspiration'), then presumably they could not firmly believe any of the other tenets. Indeed, when they hold that the defensibility of Christian tenets must rest squarely on the historical reliability of the Bible, many fundamentalists are presuming that the entire Bible is free from error ('inerrant' or 'infallible'). Belief in Biblical inerrancy might, then, be viewed as the common denominator of most fundamentalists, and that belief sets the context in which we discuss 'fundamentalists' and 'fundamentalism'.

On the basis of the belief in Biblical inerrancy, one might say that a Christian fundamentalist could also be a Mormon or a Jehovah's Witness, an Evangelical, Pentecostal, or Charismatic Christian (all of whom recognize the final authority of the Bible), or a member of *any* Protestant denomination, or the Catholic church. It may not be unusual indeed for members of an Evangelical church, for example, to identify themselves also as 'fundamentalists' to signify their belief in the infallibility of the Bible.*

The authors realize that any attempt to define a group of people or their beliefs is often fraught with danger, all too easily inviting biases, prejudices, and deception. They hope that the acceptance of a broad description might reduce if not avoid the frequently hostile and confusing debates about the 'essence' of fundamentalism, and promote a clearer view of a complex phenomenon.

By using an overspecific description, important aspects of an issue can be missed and others exaggerated. When fundamentalists are perceived simply and solely as a closed, unapproachable, blind, and unsophisticated group, one's fullest possible understanding of them becomes severely limited, bi-

---

* In North America today, most people who call themselves fundamentalist also call themselves evangelical. 'Evangelical' means 'of the Gospel'. 'Evangelical Christians' are therefore 'Gospel Christians'. The term 'evangelical' is commonly used to denote the 'born-again' variety of Protestantism, which is also fundamentalist in the sense of believing that the Bible is infallible. (In other countries, such as Germany, the word 'evangelical' has taken on a very different meaning.) However, *all* Christian churches, from Roman Catholic to Mormon, claim to be evangelical (and also 'born-again', though most churches don't interpret this as a subjective emotional experience). 'Pentecostal' churches, such as the Assemblies of God (with which the Reverend Jimmy Swaggart was once associated) are always both 'evangelical' and fundamentalist, but they have distinctive beliefs different from other evangelicals and fundamentalists. Pentecostals place special emphasis on the gift of the Holy Spirit, and therefore practice 'speaking in tongues' and other forms of worship which to non-Pentecostals seem unruly. 'Charismatics' are like Pentecostals in emphasizing direct emotional experience. But Charismatics are active in many denominations, including the Roman Catholic Church, and many Charismatics are decidedly *not* fundamentalist.

ased, and confused. With a more flexible description, the readers are provided with a broader array of considerations, more room for honest thought and exploration. Fundamentalists are demystified, and their significance is better understood.

With this description the fundamentalist becomes real and personalized, not a single-minded machine, and problems associated with fundamentalism can be seen in degrees rather then absolute terms. Given that broad understanding, an important difference between fundamentalists and many non-fundamentalists may be that the non-fundamentalists can try to understand the Bible without viewing its 'perfection' or 'imperfection' as religiously central. Yet the line that distinguishes fundamentalists from non-fundamentalists is sometimes blurry. Often people who are not especially 'devout' or 'religious' do not consider themselves to be fundamentalists, but many of them may share a fundamentalist perception of the Bible, or at least particular parts of the Bible. There are, in short, degrees of conservatism in fundamentalism, and the rest of this book will attempt to guide readers to a clearer understanding of where hazards may exist according to the degree to which one holds certain fundamentalist approaches to life and the Bible.

CHAPTER 2

Fundamentalists who have suffered

Even the most sincere and loving fundamentalists can be hurt if their religious experiences turn from being uplifting to being belittling. Many antagonists of fundamentalism point to 'emotionally disturbed' ex-fundamentalists to 'prove' that fundamentalism is inherently dangerous and causes emotional trauma to almost anyone who adheres to it. Such oversimplicity and exaggeration, unfortunately, do little to identify, much less solve, any real problems, and are often dismissed by the claim that these disaffected fundamentalists represent a disturbed minority who are unable properly to understand and apply fundamentalist principles.

It is unfair to judge any movement, ideology, or theology solely on the basis of the difficulties that some of its adherents may have in adapting to 'canonical' beliefs. Yet while it does little good to present sensational, worst-scenario examples of some fundamentalists' problems, it would also be unfair to ignore their cries without clearly examining the most likely reasons for their behavior. By trying to identify underlying causes of stress among disaffected fundamentalists, both fundamentalists and non-fundamentalists can better understand themselves and one another.

Negative Motives of Some Fundamentalists

It is true that fundamentalists who take up fundamentalism for undesirable reasons, or who bring to it certain negative personality traits, often come out of it with noticeable social and psychological problems. As they withdraw themselves from their particular fundamentalist environments, and as they attempt to rid themselves of certain feelings and emotions nurtured in those environments, they experience problems perhaps as intense as any others associated with psychological trauma. Had they misused drugs, been molested, lost loved ones, witnessed a tragedy, survived a terrible accident, or discovered a shocking truth, their problems would be similar. They would be liable to exhibit denial of the real causes of their problems, place all the blame for their problems upon themselves, become severely depressed and withdrawn, be suspicious of people, especially their former friends and family, lack self-esteem, believe that they deserved whatever pain they were feeling, hold bitterness about what they consider wasted time, and have difficulty breaking former habits or erasing feelings of guilt about no longer following old rules. Why do a number of ex-fundamentalists have such problems?

Perhaps some disaffected people are seeking religious experiences to avoid trying to cope with their inadequacies. Some people adopt religious beliefs and engage in religious practices to try to make their everyday challenges disappear, to release themselves from responsibilities, both for themselves and others, to find a simple explanation for everything, and even to find justification for hating people who do not think or act in the 'right' ways or come from the 'right' social or ethnic backgrounds. Note, however, that there are also many good reasons to seek religious experiences: to gain hope and inspiration, to become a more caring person, to develop self-confidence, to find spiritual strength, to increase one's knowledge about life, to acquire a clearer understanding of one's problems, and so on.

Unfortunately, what can be very good for some people can be very bad for others. Fundamentalism, which emphasizes dogma and purports to have all the answers necessary for this life and the afterlife, may tend to reinforce the negative motives for which some people join fundamentalist churches. Thus, while fundamentalism can nurture the noblest motives of some of its followers, it can—especially in particularly intense religious environments—also encourage the lesser motives and even insecurities of other followers.

WHAT FORMER FUNDAMENTALISTS FEEL

While many if not most fundamentalists derive comfort and meaning from their beliefs, some fundamentalists evidently feel that their beliefs and attitudes have harmed them psychologically. Among this latter group, the most visible are the members of an organization called Fundamentalists Anonymous (F.A.), details of which are given in an appendix at the end of this book.

One of its co-founders, Richard Yao, himself a former fundamentalist, says that F.A. is open to anyone who identifies with the word 'fundamentalist', but the organization is not intended for those who are happy with their religious experience. Yao believes that at least six million out of an estimated sixty million fundamentalists in the U.S.A. want to break away from their fundamentalist beliefs and environments.

Many members of F.A. maintain that a number of doctrines and rules associated with their fundamentalist churches promoted a sense of helplessness in themselves, and that this feeling was reinforced by fundamentalist teachings that self-reliance is an expression of arrogance.

'Susan', an F.A. member who did not wish to give her real name, said at a meeting of one of the F.A. chapters: "Fundamentalists try to keep us children in the sense that we don't have to think for ourselves. There is a format, there are rules." Susan's complaint resembles that of Brian Schick, another F.A. member at the same meeting, who said: "What gets me is that there's no idea of personal responsibility for yourself in fundamentalism. I only had the choice to do what was 'right.' It's monochromatic. I now find myself having to develop a sense of self. Before, there was absolute authority doing the thinking for me."

The authoritarian way in which many fundamentalists are taught their moral and religious values often expresses fears of individual judgment, ambivalence, and ambiguity. In his booklet, *There Is A Way Out* (New York: Luce Publications, 1983), Yao writes:

> The problem with the fundamentalist worldview is its acute inability to tolerate ambiguity and uncertainty in life, its inclination to paint everything in black and white, right and wrong, good and evil. Their worldview allows no uncertainties, no unanswered questions and no loose ends. (p. 3)

Some fundamentalists' sense of worthlessness and self-hatred, as well as dislike of 'outsiders', may also be reinforced by frequent assertions of mankind's essentially evil nature. In support of their system of values and beliefs, many fundamentalists are presented with vivid pictures of eternal torment. In the words of Nancy Williams, a daughter of a fundamentalist minister and an organizer of the Oakland, California, chapter of F.A.: "When your daddy is preaching hell from the pulpit, you're afraid that you'll be left on the planet when the blood falls and Satan establishes himself on earth. Those sermons were morbid and scared me to death because I never felt I'd be comfortably saved. I'd drown in the Lake of Fire. I felt coerced through childhood."

Exposed to warnings against theological nonconformity and taught that the world is basically evil, some fundamentalists experience a feeling of alienation. Further, their belief in the corruption of the world often stimulates other fears. F.A. member George Guzman's fundamentalist experience, for example, made him so fearful of 'contamination' by sin that he 'hid' in his apartment for a year and a half. Said Guzman: "I was scared of the 'outside world', afraid of being drawn into sin."

The comments of those and many other members illustrate well their anxiety. The comment of a former fundamentalist who appeared on a 1986 'Donahue' television show provides perhaps as poignant a view of their pain as any former fundamentalist could express. Billy Jackson told a national audience his impression of how fundamentalism had been practiced in his church: "We had to become like Jesus Christ and die to ourselves. In other words, you kill your own personality off and try and replace it with Jesus Christ. When I did leave I had killed myself off to such a point that there was nothing of me left, and that's what keeps you in there because you can't relate to anyone else."

'Lisa' was raised in a strict fundamentalist home, in which she rarely did or thought anything that diverged from the values of her parents, particularly her authoritarian father, who often subjected her to verbal abuse. When she left home to study at a fundamentalist Christian college, she tried attending various churches, but says that going to church made her feel as if "somebody had their hands on my neck. I just couldn't breathe." One time, when she was home for a holiday, and had missed going to church because she overslept, her father screamed at her, saying that she was going to Hell.

Lisa reports a long, hard battle to overcome the crippling effects of her upbringing, and sighs that "it's still not over." Her father, she says, now tells her siblings that she is "of the Devil". She attends a mainstream church, and says of herself: "Scapegoats have the best rate of recovery because they never had the luxury of pretending that everything was OK."

Ruth Schilling, now a Chicago actress, was raised by her mother and grandmother, both fundamentalists. Her grandmother, who was particularly negative and world-denying, often expressed her negativity in religious language. For example, she prayed to be taken from "this wicked world", and often said that Ruth was "of the Devil".

In high school, Ruth agonized over her inability to believe what she was expected to believe. She was given the impression that if she accepted Christ into her heart, she would have an experience after which everything would be wonderful. But instead she continued to feel "rotten", and concluded that God had not accepted her. She sometimes experienced "spiritual highs", but they never lasted.

When she left the church in her early twenties, with "nothing to go on", she was convinced that her only choice was "to be a really awful person, a criminal, or a prostitute." She became involved in the theatre, and was drawn into the easy sex and drugs scene of San Francisco in the late 1960s. She always tended to worship and follow blindly the men with whom she associated.

Now into her forties, Schilling reflects that she has spent much of her life chasing one pseudo-religion after another. She went through a period of intense self-examination, where even issues like brushing her teeth at night became momentous decisions. She looks back on such self-searching as petty and dogmatic, like her childhood training.

Barb Dyche was a churchgoing fundamentalist who got married, for the second time, to a man she met through the church. Her new husband told her to sell her house and move in with him, but not to bring along her two children, aged 20 and 22. She sought the advice of her pastor about that request. The pastor advised that a wife should submit to her husband's demands, but Barb decided to ignore this advice, and eventually her husband divorced her.

At this point, the attitude of the entire church became hostile. She was no longer allowed to sing in the choir, or play her violin in church as she had sometimes done previously. Some of the congregation attempted to discipline her by "chiding" her, once even turning up at her home to reproach and threaten her. Among their other excesses, the church members called a counsellor she was seeing, trying to make an appointment to talk about her. Naturally, the counsellor refused to do so without Barb's consent.

Barb refuses to get angry with the church members, and says that their behavior is understandable to her, though it has caused her some irritation and frustration. "I love God and I want to know him and grow in him", she says. "But I'm not so sure that what's happening in the church right now is going to help me."

We do not imply that such sad stories by fundamentalists and former fundamentalists are *typical*, but they are certainly commonplace. It is not difficult to see how fundamentalist experiences could intensify some people's negative traits almost as easily as their positive traits.

Conclusion

One might argue that the thousands of ex-fundamentalists who are suffering today were in some sense disturbed even before they became fundamentalists, that they were highly vulnerable to psychological trauma, or that, for whatever reasons, they were simply unable to grasp fundamentalism. Some would say that 'former fundamentalists' were never *really* fundamentalists, since fundamentalists, who are saved, cannot become 'unsaved'. Some may even claim that the trauma is Divine punishment for disbelief. In any case, it appears that fundamentalism, much like anything requiring the pursuit of goals that are difficult to reach, can attract some people to it who will ultimately suffer psychological problems.

Perhaps the confusion that many fundamentalists have experienced is rooted not necessarily in what particular beliefs they acquired, but rather in *how* they acquired those beliefs. As will be considered in the next chapter, no matter what teaching people may follow, if they accept that teaching without being encouraged to study it thoroughly and to seek out *many* interpretations of it, they may reach only a distorted understanding of that teaching, and may ultimately have trouble dealing with doubts, warranted or not, about its truth.

NOTE: The personal stories of 'Susan', Nancy Williams, and George Guzman were reported in 'Breaking Away: When Fundamentalists Leave the Fold', by Hilary Abramson, *Sacramento Bee Magazine*, June 22, 1986, that of Billy Jackson on the 'Donahue' show (Donahue Transcript #05075, Multimedia Entertainment, Inc.), and those of 'Lisa', Ruth Schilling, and Barb Dyche in an article by Dan Liberty in the Chicago *Reader*, March 25, 1988.

CHAPTER 3

Pat ROBERTSON AND JERRY FALWELL

Biblical inerrancy—the infallibility of the Bible—which most fundamentalists profess, is often taught in a way that gives its adherents the impression that the Bible is an *easy*-to-use guide to moral conduct, religious belief, and even everyday life. Unfortunately with such a conception, people are liable to avoid studying the Bible carefully, for they may assume that its interpretation is simple and requires little more than reading particular passages, and then applying them wherever needed. In short, they may come to equate the infallibility of the Bible with the infallibility of their interpretation of the Bible.

The Bible is, however, a complex work, and readers of the Bible can misinterpret its meaning and significance. Only when people have carefully studied the entire Bible and different interpretations of it that scholars have advanced, can they be assured that they have achieved a fair understanding of it.

Biblical scholars, whether fundamentalists or non-fundamentalists, study many aspects of the Bible, including how the Bible relates to the world around them. In fact, they feel required to read as much of the latest scholarly literature pertaining to Biblical criticism as possible. They know that such knowledge allows them more fully to understand their own beliefs by better understanding the arguments being advanced against those beliefs. They also find some comfort in believing that their views have stood the test of comparison with opposing viewpoints. Accordingly, while many fundamentalists may think that it is sinful to study beliefs that are opposed to their own, fundamentalist scholars, in fact, do that often. In other words, one can be a fundamentalist and still read books, such as this one, that may discuss other points of view.

Yet when conservative evangelists ignore or minimize the difficulties in interpreting Scripture and sometimes present themselves in effect as Divine prophets, their followers may believe not only that study of the Bible from all possible points of view is unnecessary but also that the evangelists' teachings should be accepted as true only because the particular evangelists vouch for those teachings. As a result, the followers may come to hold beliefs without satisfying their natural curiosity about how the beliefs were established and what other beliefs exist. They may even come to avoid listening to or studying other viewpoints, fearing that they might discover something in the Bible that may seem 'false'.

Consider, for example, some of the teachings of two major conservative evangelists, M. G. 'Pat' Robertson (former minister at the Christian Broadcasting Network) and Jerry Falwell. The point here is not either to condone or condemn their beliefs. Rather, the point is to consider whether their teachings may be leading their followers to take an oversimple view of the Bible, a view that tends to depreciate the necessity for careful study of many diverse beliefs and concepts.

Please look, first, at some of the Reverend Falwell's teachings as they are expounded in his *Finding Inner Peace and Strength* (Garden City, N.Y.: Doubleday, 1982), and then examine some of Pat Robertson's teachings as expounded in his *Answers to 200 of Life's Most Probing Questions* (Nashville: Thomas Nelson, 1985).

Jerry Falwell

1. The Reverend Falwell teaches that the Bible is inerrant. He says:

> The Bible is the inerrant, . . . Word of the living God. It is absolutely infallible, without error in all matters pertaining to faith and practice, as well as in areas such as geography, science, history, etc. (*Finding Inner Peace and Strength*, p. 26)

> The Bible is without error. . . . There is no mixture of error to be found within its pages. The Bible is the only perfectly divine thing on this earth. . . . (p. 129)

Followers of that teaching may tend to avoid studying any research that suggests the possibility of the existence of pre-scientific thought (see our Chapter 5 for a detailed discussion of that possibility) or a gradual development of moral codes (see Chapter 6) expressed in the Bible, a human side of the Biblical Jesus (see Chapter 7), or any difficulties with some New Testament interpretations of Old Testament verses (see Chapter 10). Further, uncritical followers may be liable to accept popular misconceptions about the Bible concerning its originality, authorship, accuracy, et cetera (see Chapter 8).

2. The Reverend Falwell teaches that the Bible is the inspired Word of God:

> The Bible is the . . . inspired Word of the living God. (p. 26)

> The Holy Spirit declares that the Bible is God's Word. . . . The Scriptures were inspired by God. . . . They find their source in God Himself. This is why we hold the Bible in such reverence. We accept its claim to be the Word of God. (p. 126)

> Jesus was the living Word, and the Bible is the written Word. God desired that men and women know the reason for their existence—the why, the how, the when, etc.—so He gave man His Word. . . . (p. 129)

Followers of the Reverend Falwell's view on inspiration may tend to avoid considering the arguments of anyone who might point out that the Bible lacks any statement clearly indicating that the entire Bible is directly inspired (see Chapter 8).

3. The Reverend Falwell teaches that what is written in the Bible is useful for all time, its laws immutable:

> It [the Bible] is the everlasting Word that has never [changed] and will never know change. . . .
> . . . although this is a clever generation, it is one that is suffering because men are . . . disregarding God's immutable laws. . . . [and] disobeying the clear instructions God gave in His Word. (p. 26)

> The Bible is truly the foundation upon which the Christian faith rests. It should be the blueprint for your life. (p. 126)

> This is a changing world. But how wonderful it is to have a Book that never changes. The Bible is just as relevant today as it was when it was written. (p. 128)

> Not only does it [the Bible] contain the truthful answers to life's most important questions, but it gives answers to hundreds of other questions as well that affect our daily lives. And when questions arise that are not directly addressed, we are left with principles to use as guidelines for determining the answers. (pp. 129–30)

Followers of that teaching often treat all Biblical rules as 'perfect', and therefore eternally useful, and do not usually consider that some of those rules could, perhaps, be barbarous or impractical today (see Chapter 6). They may not fully appreciate that Jesus himself opposed, or at least questioned, popular interpretations of some of the Mosaic laws (see Chapter 9).

4. The Reverend Falwell teaches that the writings within the Bible are all in agreement, uncontradictory, and of singular direction and clarity:

> Forty men, over a period of sixteen hundred years, . . . wrote the Bible under the inspiration of the Holy Spirit. Many of those forty men knew none of the others, yet their writings are in agreement. There is harmony, unity, centrality of theme, . . . (p. 126)

Followers of that teaching of the Reverend Falwell may tend not to appreciate fully the diversity of belief expressed in the Bible (see our discussion, 'Does the Bible Present a Single Viewpoint?' in Chapter 8). They may also tend to avoid studying any research that might suggest that most of the Bible evolved through multiple authorship and complex editing (see Chapter 11).

5. The Reverend Falwell teaches that Jesus was perfect, indeed Divine, and that God therefore accepts the blood sacrifice of Jesus as full atonement for humankind's sins:

> The deity of Jesus Christ is the cornerstone of the Christian faith. (p. 24)

> [Jesus Christ] was the God-man on this earth—perfect God and perfect man. (p. 24)

> Only because He was God incarnate could Jesus Christ die a vicarious death for the sins of the world. He could never have taken upon Himself the sins of all humanity unless He was God in the flesh. . . .
> Through His voluntary death on the cross, Jesus Christ, who knew no sin, was made sin for man. He had satisfied the just requirements of the perfect, righteous nature of God. . . .

A sinless blood sacrifice was required because there is life only in the blood. "For the life of the flesh is in the blood . . . for it is the blood that maketh an atonement for the soul" (Lev. 17:11).

His [God's] righteousness had to be satisfied through the cross before man could be reconciled to Him because God cannot look upon sin. (pp. 51–52)

Followers of that teaching of the Reverend Falwell may tend not to study the moral questions arising from some of the actions and statements ascribed to Jesus (see Chapter 7). They also might tend to be reluctant to read carefully those portions of the Bible (for example, Isaiah 1:11–17) that portray God as being sated with ritual blood sacrifices and as desiring only that people learn to do good and cease to do evil (see Chapter 7).

6. The Reverend Falwell teaches that Jesus is "the way" and that people who do not accept Jesus as their Lord are in danger of failure and eternal damnation:

In John 14:6 Jesus Christ said, "I am the way." He did not say that He was a way among ways; He said, "I am the way, the truth, and the life." (p. 46)

If you are not a Christian, it is truly a sad thing. It is sad because one day you will meet God, unprepared, and spend eternity in hell. (p. 27)

If your purpose in life is anything but the glory of the Lord Jesus Christ, you are going to fail miserably, and you are going to be unhappy with God in the process. (p. 31)

I can think of many who, because of neglecting a personal relationship with Christ will live, die, and spend eternity in a Christless hell. (p. 41)

Hell is a place of undiluted divine wrath. . . . God's final wrath will not be mixed with mercy. . . .
Hell is a place created for all eternity. . . . In other words, hell will continue as long as God's works continue, which is forever. . . . (pp. 42–43)

That teaching, however, may tend to discourage people from considering any moral questions associated with infinite punishment for finite crimes (see Chapter 7). Further, while they might not ever condone religious intolerance or

cite the Bible to justify such intolerance, those followers may
tend to avoid studying any historical research that might indicate that the belief in damnation for religious disbelief has, at
times, led some people to condone religious intolerance, justi-
fying their behavior by citing the Bible (see Chapter 9).

7. The Reverend Falwell teaches that the Virgin Birth
claim must be true, or else the entire Bible would be a lie and
Jesus could not be the world's Saviour:

> It is important to recognize that Mary was a virgin. If Christ had not
> been born of a virgin, the Bible would be a lie. If He had had a human
> father and if His mother had been an illicit woman, then He by nature
> would have inherited the fallen disposition of His earthly father and
> would have needed someone to save Him. He certainly could not have
> been the Saviour of the world. (p. 47)

Followers of that teaching may tend to avoid reading any
books that discuss the Biblical evidence that Paul, Mark,
John, and Jesus were silent about the spectacular birth (see
Chapter 11). They may also tend to be overcautious about
examining any historical evidence that points out that the
Virgin Birth claim put forth by Matthew appears to have
been based on an inaccurate translation, and that virgin
births are foreign to the Old Testament (see Chapter 10).
Further, those followers may become unwilling to study any
research that suggests all the reasons that might have motivated the Virgin Birth claim (see Chapter 11). The Reverend
Falwell's teaching also tends to encourage people to believe
that there is only one way to perceive the Bible: that it must
be totally worthless if it is found to contain even one inconsistency (see Chapter 4).

8. The Reverend Falwell teaches that the New Testament
contains much fulfilled prophecy from the Old Testament:

> I believe the Bible is God's Word also because of fulfilled prophecy.
> Dozens of predictions were made in the Old Testament that were ful-
> filled in the New Testament in every detail. There are so many cases of
> fulfilled prophecies in the Bible that only the atheist or agnostic would
> believe them to be merely coincidental. Over two dozen prophecies
> have been fulfilled relating to the death, burial, and resurrection of
> Christ alone. At least twelve of these are found in the fifty-third
> chapter of Isaiah, which was written seven hundred years before

Christ was born! Fulfilled prophecy is an undisputable evidence that
the Bible was written under the inspiration of the Holy Spirit.
(pp. 126–27)

That teaching may have the effect of discouraging uncritical followers from recognizing the occasions when New
Testament authors most likely misconstrued the meanings
of Old Testament verses. Those followers may often avoid
studying any evidence put forth by scholars who might
claim that, since some New Testament writers were dedi-
cated to proving that Jesus fulfilled all the Old Testament
Messianic predictions, the authors sometimes may have
misunderstood the context of Old Testament verses that
they perhaps honestly believed were fulfilled prophecies.
(See Chapters 10 and 11.)

9. The Reverend Falwell teaches that, at least in the spiritual sense, God does not want people to be self-reliant, or to
have much self-esteem:

Start your day off by ridding yourself of self-reliance. (p. 15)

Only as we reach a point of total helplessness and recognize that we
can do nothing for God, that only as He lives His life out through us as
we totally depend on Him, will we know peace and victory in the
Christian life. (p. 93)

. . . if we are to be obedient in carrying out the marching orders that
God has given to every believer, we must be in total agreement with
God. He must be our all and obedience to Him and His Word our primary objective in life. We must be nothing in order that He might be
everything.
No amount of self-determination can ever change you. Change will
come only as you reckon yourself dead in Christ to the areas of your
weakness and yield to the Holy Spirit. . . . You will only become like
Jesus Christ as you learn that you are totally dependent upon Him for
your very life.
When self is on the throne of your life . . . you will manifest . . . self-
sufficiency. . . . All this kind of self-manifestation grieves God. It reveals that you are not depending on Him every hour that you live.
(pp. 114–15)

When a man sees himself as a depraved, unrighteous, hell-
deserving sinner with the blood of the cross on his hands, he is in a position to be eternally changed. (p. 65)

> A child has to depend on someone else for its needs and that is just what attitude a man must have toward Christ. (p. 67)

> Today Christ delights in those meek persons who humbly serve Him as bondslaves. (p. 112)

Unfortunately, any teaching of helplessness is often also attractive to people who are seeking justification for their failures. Followed uncritically, therefore, the Reverend Falwell's teaching on dependency may tend to encourage helpless-feeling people to interpret the Bible in such ways as to justify their feeling of helplessness and thus fulfill their psychological need for avoiding self-reliance. For while such a need is hardly productive, it is often easier to stay poor, incompetent, and dependent in life than to try to be rich, competent, and independent. Confessing and endorsing incompetence and helplessness protects people from the dangers of failure inherent in high expectations. As the saying goes, he who is down need not fear a fall.

Thus, for example, such self-depreciating people may read 2 Corinthians 12:9–11, in which, to them, Paul may seem to be describing how God made him happy to be emotionally, intellectually, and physically weak:

> Each time he [God] said, ". . . I am with you, that is all you need. My power shows up best in weak people." Now I am glad to boast about how weak I am; I am glad to be a living demonstration of Christ's power, instead of showing off my own power and abilities. Since I know it is all for Christ's good, I am quite happy about "the thorn," and about insults and hardships, persecutions and difficulties; for when I am weak, then I am strong—the less I have, the more I depend on him. . . .
> I am really worth nothing at all.

They may, however dubiously, also tend to interpret certain verses in the Bible as saying that God does not favor free, autonomous adults, but rather prefers sheep (John 10:11, 15), children (Matthew 18:3), slaves (Matthew 6:24), and fools (1 Corinthians 4:10).

Further, they may, perhaps dubiously, view Jesus' Sermon on the Mount as endorsing their feelings of helplessness. For in the Sermon, as presented by Luke, Jesus blesses the poor (Luke 6:20), the hungry (6:21), the mournful (6:21), and the persecuted (6:22), while he seems to condemn the rich (6:24), the "fat and prosperous" (6:25), the joyful (6:25), and the admired (6:26).

Indeed, for at least some people, especially those who consider themselves incompetent or helpless, Jesus' statement that the first shall be last and the last shall be first (Matthew 19:30) is joyfully taken as proclaiming that this-worldly winners will become losers in the next world, and that this-worldly *losers* will become winners.

If, therefore, some uncritical followers of the Reverend Falwell's teachings are led to believe that they can use the Bible to satisfy some of their least productive psychological needs, then they may be liable to become, in a sense, psychologically dependent on the Biblical interpretations that satisfy those needs. Yet when people become psychologically dependent on particular interpretations, they are often only a small step away from becoming so dependent on those interpretations that they could be shattered psychologically if they ever concluded that the Bible is not utterly free from error. In other words, they may come to fear that if *any* part of the Bible is errant, then the parts of the Bible that they depend on might also be in error; and thus their justification for their supposed shortcomings, failures, and helplessness might crumble.

PAT ROBERTSON

Consider now some of the teachings of Pat Robertson as they are explained in his *Answers to 200 of Life's Most Probing Questions*.

1. Pat Robertson teaches that the Bible should be people's primary spiritual guide. He says:

> God's primary means for giving us guidance is the Bible. The Bible is our rulebook of faith and practice. . . . He [God] never guides His people contrary to the clear principles of His written Word. (*Answers to 200 of Life's Most Probing Questions*, p. 216)

> [T]he spiritual standard for America . . . [should be] the gospel of Jesus and everything in the New and Old Testaments. (p. 87)

That teaching of Pat Robertson may tend to give his followers the impression that the Bible is an *easy* guide to everyday living, containing essentially no inconsistencies (see our discussion, 'Is the Bible Perfectly Accurate?' in Chapter 8). Uncritical followers, therefore, sometimes may not fully appreciate the complexity of the Bible, and may tend to avoid studying any aspects of its diversity of beliefs (see 'Does the Bible Present a Single Viewpoint?' in Chapter 8, below), its patterns of moral development (see Chapter 6), its pre-scientific methods (see Chapter 5), its depiction of Jesus as sometimes perhaps being human enough to make mistakes (see Chapter 7), and its occasionally surprising interpretations of Old Testament verses advanced by New Testament authors (see Chapter 10). The followers may also tend to neglect alerting themselves to the ways in which the Bible has in the past sometimes been misused, even by the most devout and knowledgeable people, as a tool for hatred and persecution (see Chapter 9).

2. Pat Robertson teaches that Jesus is perfect, and that he fulfilled Old Testament Messianic prophecies of virgin birth and Davidic descent:

> Jesus Christ was the only perfect man who ever lived,. . . (p. 22)

> The Bible teaches that He was truly God from the moment of His conception by the Holy Spirit. (p. 69)

> The Bible says in Isaiah that God would give us a sign: "The virgin shall conceive and bear a Son." The word in Hebrew that we translate as "virgin" is *almah*, and it can mean "virgin" or "young woman." The word has been translated "virgin," however, because there is nothing unusual about a young woman giving birth, so that would be no sign at all. (p. 67)

> Linking Jesus into the family tree of Mary, however, made Him a descendant of David and Abraham, which fulfilled the various promises that God had made to them. (p. 68)

That teaching may tend to discourage its followers from studying carefully any verse that may suggest the possibility of even very minor flaws in either the character or teachings of the Biblical Jesus (see Chapter 7). Further, by judging Jesus' Messiahship mainly on the basis of New Testament claims, uncritical followers may be unwilling to study any research that considers whether misinterpretations about Messianic prophecy could exist in the New Testament (see Chapter 10). They may also not think seriously about any historical influence that could have been acting upon the New Testament writers (see Chapter 11).

3. Pat Robertson teaches that people must have faith in Jesus to be saved from Hell and sometimes from even this-worldly punishment:

> Everyone must be born again before he or she can enter heaven. (p. 161)

> To be saved you must turn away from sin, believe in the death and resurrection of Jesus, and receive Him as Lord and Savior of your life. . . . (p. 82)

> The Bible says no one can become worthy of God's blessings through trying to be better,. . . . Ephesians 2:8–9 reads, "For by grace you have been saved through faith, and that not of yourselves; it is the gift of God, not of works, lest anyone should boast." (p. 39)

> . . . Israel was destroyed and its people scattered abroad because of their unbelief. (p. 147)

> Human beings were never intended to go into hell. But the ones who choose to reject God will one day follow Satan right into hell.
> There will be no exit from hell, no way out, no second chance. That is why it is so important in this life to receive the pardon that God extends to all men through the cross of Jesus Christ. (p. 160)

Followers of that teaching may tend to avoid considering the intolerance of such a restriction upon the availability of salvation (see Chapter 7). They may also tend to avoid learning about the ways in which that restriction has perhaps sometimes been used by people to 'justify' their hatred towards non-Christians (see Chapter 9).

4. Pat Robertson teaches that, according to the Bible, God rules only by love and encourages independence:

> If God just reached out with His power and struck Satan, other created beings could say He did it because He could not win by love, and so He had to resort to force and fear. (p. 48)

> The person who is victimized by fear should . . . memorize and recite the Word of God,. . .
> . . . this rebuke[s] the spirit of fear and Satan who brings it,. . .
> Perfect love casts out fear. . . . (p. 229)

[In contradistinction to Christianity] cults frequently attempt to instill fear into their followers. The followers are taught constantly that salvation comes only through the cult. "If you leave us, you will lose your salvation," they say. (p. 135)

Followers of that teaching of Pat Robertson may tend to dismiss without careful study the apparent use of force and deception found in some parts of the Old Testament (see Chapter 6). They are also unlikely to appreciate fully the intimidation involved in the notion of losing salvation and suffering eternal damnation for certain kinds of disbelief (see Chapters 2 and 7).

CONCLUSION

If people choose to follow the teachings of Jerry Falwell, Pat Robertson, or any other evangelist who may tend to present the Bible as inerrantly reflecting the will of God, they might do well also to explore in greater depth those teachings as well as other viewpoints. For by better understanding the beliefs of others, people's own beliefs can be refined and honed, their sensitivity to others increased, and their appreciation of the Bible strengthened by an awareness of Biblical inconsistencies and implausibilities and their possible explanations.

Thus far, it has been shown how negative personality traits may be reinforced, intentionally or not, by certain fundamentalist experiences, and how the tendency to avoid careful and thoughtful study of one's religious beliefs may be promoted, also perhaps unintentionally, by certain teachings of conservative evangelists. The next chapter will examine the underlying doctrine from which those and other potential hazards in Christian fundamentalism often spring.

CHAPTER 4

T HE BIBLE: IS IT INFALLIBLE?

A n understanding of the hazards in Christian fundamentalism is unattainable without a basic knowledge of the doctrine of Biblical inerrancy.* Many fundamentalists' principal approach to the Bible is based on the assumption that this doctrine is true. This chapter will consider that assumption, by examining some of the major reasons that some people are attracted to the doctrine, while others are repelled by it. In later chapters we discuss specific examples of inconsistencies or inaccuracies in the Bible.

WHAT IS THE DOCTRINE OF BIBLICAL INERRANCY?
The doctrine of Biblical inerrancy, as it is adopted by most fundamentalists, essentially maintains that the entire Bible was dictated, word for word, directly from God to the Biblical writers, and that because it was all dictated by God it must all be true, completely free from error (inerrant). While those inerrantists may allow for flexibility in their interpretation of certain verses—viewing them sometimes as, for example, allegory, symbolism , or poetry—and while some inerrantist theologians may advance such adaptations, especially when faced with difficulties in some interpretations, they will still hold the presumption of the inerrancy of the Bible, and try never to sway from that presumption. (A discussion of some

---

*In many non-technical usages the terms 'inerrant' and 'infallible' are interchangeable, both referring to exemption from error. Although we use these terms interchangeably in this book, they also have technical usages among some religious groups. For example, among some groups the term 'infallible' refers to the absolute trustworthiness of Scripture only in its teachings and doctrines, particularly those bearing on salvation. Among some other groups, the term 'inerrancy' is applied only to the original Biblical manuscripts (autographs), which are no longer available.

of the adaptations to the doctrine of Biblical inerrancy advanced by some fundamentalist and evangelical theologians is contained in Chapter 12 of this book.)

WHAT ARE ITS ATTRACTIONS?

Fundamentalists normally do not treat the doctrine of inerrancy as simply one explanation among others for the nature of the Bible. Rather, to them, the doctrine of inerrancy is more like an unquestionable law than an explanatory theory. So treated, the doctrine leads most fundamentalists to feel confident that each Biblical verse can be easily understood and applied to life's problems. Fundamentalists view the Bible as the final authority on all matters of importance in their life, and many believe that it is reliable only if it is entirely inerrant. Their approach to the Bible directly affects their views not only on obviously religious matters but on *all* matters. The well-publicized views, for example, of many fundamentalists on such topics as abortion, pornography, the family, humanism, school prayer, censorship, homosexuality, church-state relations, Communism, and national defense will not be discussed in this book, but all such views are, in their eyes, dictated in large part by their approach to the Bible. Fundamentalists, therefore, rest both their faith in God and their understandings about the world squarely upon their view of the Bible as an inerrant work.

It is, then, the apparent simplicity of Biblical inerrancy that is appealing to many fundamentalists, and that simplicity is basic to their approach not only to the Bible but also to the world around them. To many people, the doctrine of Biblical inerrancy and the fundamentalist system of thought in which it is embedded are enormously attractive. Intellectual systems generally, with their consequent orderliness, are often attractive because they help people to generalize about their experiences and the world. Indeed, thinking and talking about what one has not experienced on the basis of what one has experienced is indispensable to any abstract thinking, including scientific thinking. Scientists appeal to various canons of reasoning to predict the future on the basis of the past. For example, they talk about 'all zebras' on the basis of such zebras as have been studied.

Systems of thought that generalize about the world, then, can simplify, or at least seem to simplify, an otherwise chaotic world. The doctrine of Biblical inerrancy, however, does not exist by itself within that system. Fundamentalist teachings and fundamentalist environments, which, as discussed in the two previous chapters, often tend to discourage or minimize the importance of careful study of various Biblical interpretations, are also part of the fundamentalists' approach. Viewing the Bible as totally free from error *and* keeping any doubts about that doctrine out of mind, is an attractive approach for many people.

A system of thought that denounces all alternative ways of thinking is often enormously attractive, especially in times of widespread moral and religious uncertainty. It offers an anchor in the whirlpool of cultural change. By requiring uncritical acceptance of black-and-white definitions, such systems of thought can appeal to millions of people, who find ambiguity and ambivalence disturbing. People rarely want to admit to others or even to themselves that there are many different ways of looking at and evaluating their most treasured beliefs. It is far easier for people to believe that their way of thinking is *the* way, and that all other understandings must be misunderstandings.

WHAT ARE ITS DRAWBACKS?

It must be pointed out that, even though fundamentalists' approach to the Bible typically imparts oversimple answers, the people who adopt the doctrine of inerrancy are *not* stupid. In fact, the doctrine often functions within a system of thought that possesses a considerable degree of logical coherence, though it is a logic that is often opposed to modern scientific methods (a fact that many fundamentalists readily acknowledge). Nonetheless, there are serious moral and intellectual problems with the doctrine of inerrancy. It is false to the Bible, to science, and perhaps even to the idea of a good Creator.

The most serious problem with the fundamentalists' approach to the Bible may not necessarily be that it affirms the inerrancy of the Bible. Rather, the most serious problem with it is perhaps that it is preoccupied with the issue of inerrancy in the first place. Such a preoccupation with the issue of inerrancy reflects an understanding that probably would not be found even in most atheists. 'Either the Bible is without error or it is morally and religiously worthless.' By thinking in those polarities, many fundamentalists subscribe to a system of thought that often distorts Scripture and contradicts science.

The Bible, in fact, nowhere directly states that all of it is inerrant. Even if there is some verse that remotely suggests that idea, it is just that: a remote suggestion. The point is that the Bible is certainly not preoccupied with its inerrancy—it does not even appear to mention it. It seems, indeed, that God would most likely prefer that people use their critical minds to study His words rather than that people risk misunderstanding those words by simply assuming something to be true that might not be true.

POTENTIAL INTELLECTUAL DIFFICULTIES WITH BIBLICAL INERRANCY

The intellectual difficulties associated with the doctrine of Biblical inerrancy lie not in its adherents' generalizations *per se* but rather in the unwillingness of its adherents to abandon certain generalizations in the face of contrary evidence. While reasonable generalizations can often make confusing things easier to understand, some generalizations oversimplify and distort the world to make it mesh with oversimple expectations. Many components of racial prejudice, for example, arise from uncritical acceptance of stereotypical overgeneralizations. Indeed, by overgeneralizing and not questioning assumptions and definitions, entire systems of thought can inadequately describe the world and fail to do justice to its complexity. Perhaps the most tragic example of oversimplified thought is Naziism, which relied on uncritical definitions of Jews and the uncritical acceptance of the idea of the Germans' being a chosen people.

In some ways, the doctrine of Biblical inerrancy forces its adherents needlessly to contradict science. Note that while the claims of many archaeologists, historians, and Biblical scholars often trouble fundamentalists, many other people do not feel that their faith is threatened by such claims, or that they must defend their faith in the face of those claims. Many fundamentalists, however, feel impelled to attack the claim, for example, that the Israelites under Joshua most likely did not conquer the city of Ai (contrary to Joshua 7:1–8:29), which archaeological evidence suggests was not occupied during Joshua's lifetime. They feel that their faith is directly threatened also when, for example, scientific data reveal that the Philistines did not enter Canaan until about 1150 B.C., about five hundred years later than the period usually associated with Abraham, whom the Bible claims spent much time in the "land of the Philistines" (Genesis 21:34). Finally, when Biblical scholars and ethicists point out, for example, Biblical expressions of racial prejudice, as in the anti-Canaanite sentiment found in Genesis 9:18–27, many fundamentalists must defend those sentiments as inerrantly expressing God's will and thus proper.

Unlike fundamentalists, many of whom have historically been opposed to the findings of science, many other religious people can appreciate that the Bible reflects, for example, a pre-scientific view of astronomy, geology, and nature generally. Quite understandably, the Biblical writers, like most people of their day, described the world largely as it appeared to their senses, and their speculation, judged by current standards, was for the most part scientifically unsophisticated. The entire Bible adopts a cosmology that most ancient people, like most medieval people, used to describe the world. (For a discussion of this subject, see Chapter 5.) Most non-fundamentalists do not feel that their faith in God or their ability to use the Bible is at all hampered by acknowledging the pre-scientific background of the Bible.

Yet most believers in Biblical inerrancy feel impelled to view the entire Bible as scientifically accurate, even those parts that may not be consistent with present scientific knowledge.

MORAL DIFFICULTIES WITH BIBLICAL INERRANCY

One reason some religious people have criticized the fundamentalists' approach to the Bible is that they believe that it insults man and is unworthy of God. The primary importance of the Bible lies not in the presence or absence of scientific and historical errors, but in its capacity to be a source for moral and spiritual growth.

Conflicting moral views, however, are advanced in different parts of the Bible, and they cannot be fully resolved with the assumption of inerrancy. In some parts, for example, God is pictured as partial and vengeful (see Chapter 6 for a number of examples), and sometimes, therefore, the view that all people are equally important and equally worthy of moral consideration is foreign to parts of the Bible. Those examples of limited moral concern, however, contrast sharply with other parts of the Bible, covering, for instance, the times of the later prophets and Jesus, who taught universal love and universal moral concern. The moral concern of the Hebrews was a hard-won insight whose progress the Bible demonstrates magnificently. Yet applying the doctrine of Biblical inerrancy, people are required somehow to accept such divergent moral viewpoints. The result usually distorts the moral value of the Bible and ultimately the view of God's morality.

ANOTHER APPROACH TO THE BIBLE
The Bible nowhere describes Biblical authors as being made temporarily perfect or infallible for the purpose of writing the Bible while at all other times being, like most people, imperfect and fallible. Even if such exceptional occurrences did take place, it would be puzzling to many people. For why would God take control of the Biblical writers, temporarily making them infallible, displacing their humanity, and using them as mechanical mouthpieces, dictating to them exactly what they had to say and write, when He surely must have a number of other methods of communicating that would be more sensitive to the human intelligence? God has, indeed, provided mankind with an excellent source of inspiration and guidance in the form of the Bible, but it is of maximum usefulness only when people use their minds, which He created, to decide what is probably true, and what is probably not true.

That some fundamentalist teachings and environments often tend to discourage careful study of various interpretations further compounds potential intellectual difficulties. If people who adopt the doctrine of inerrancy are inquisitive about other points of view, then they can at least be cautious about those verses, laws, principles, beliefs, or interpretations that may contradict their own reasonable, and morally acceptable, judgments. They can try to avoid those ideas, even if they still do not want to stop viewing the Bible as theoretically inerrant. Yet because of the opposition to thinking about other viewpoints, many people do not exercise such critical thought.

At least one Biblical scholar who does not adopt the doctrine of Biblical inerrancy makes the following observations. His words certainly do not express the *only* possible viewpoint, but they do serve to illustrate another approach that many people may find helpful:

> Is one to take historical error, limited scientific knowledge, and human prejudice as indication of divine dictation or as a clear sign that man himself is the author and interpreter of the materials? Obviously, the latter is preferable, for it is . . . in this choice that one avoids a problematic view of God and a demeaning portrait of man. . . . [I]n this perspective . . . man become[s] a meaningful, self-determining agent rather than a puppet. And if the Biblical record is clear on any point, it is that man was created to be a free agent capable of choice and determination.
>
> Thus much depends on our basic attitude toward the Bible, how we would describe the volume as a literary product. *The Bible is man's understanding of his encounter with God.* In such a view the integrity of both God and man are preserved [and] the record [is] consistent with its evolution, transmission, and ultimate canonical status. (Frank Eakin, Jr., *Religion in Western Culture*, pp. 24–25)

THE ULTIMATE CONCERN

People may disagree with that view, but one thing must be said: In their search for the messages of God or truth in anything, people must not limit themselves to one, fixed approach that supposedly reaches 'the truth', while it denies the possibility of many other avenues to, and forms of, truth. People may have found truth in the Bible by studying it as history, as literature, as myth, as symbol, or even as science or literal truth; but whichever path they have taken, they should try to be as honest, sensitive, and thoughtful as they can.

Most fundamentalists are pursuers of truth. They show moral courage. They want to preserve the family unit. They want their children to be loving people who do not harm themselves and who always respect others. They want to keep alive the freshness of the Christian message, especially to love thy neighbor, to resist temptations to be unkind, and to turn the other cheek when harmed by others. They give to charity, and encourage others to do likewise. They worry about sexual promiscuity, hunger, sickness, drug abuse, and other problems. They are devoted to their beliefs, and they are prepared to state their views and to hold fast to them, even when these may be unpopular.

Yet with all of these excellent qualities acknowledged, the doctrine of Biblical inerrancy is nonetheless, in effect, an intellectually incomplete approach to truth. Fundamentalists may have discovered truth through the good things that they do and the kind thoughts that they carry in their hearts, but it is questionable whether their approach to the Bible is a completely fair, sensitive, and honest approach to God or truth. Since most fundamentalists believe that any Biblical 'error' is incompatible with Divine perfection, they cannot allow anything to count as a Biblical inconsistency or implausibility. Such an unquestioned presupposition, however, is not most likely a product of impartial research.

CONCLUSION

The doctrine of Biblical inerrancy is fraught with intellectual difficulties. Further, fundamentalists who choose to hold the doctrine of inerrancy face the serious hazard of being unable to recognize and acknowledge whatever inconsistencies may exist in the Bible.

Yet the Bible has a rich diversity of understanding, ranging from the cosmology of the universe to the morality of its times and cultures, and it has, therefore, many sources of potential inconsistencies. In the face of numerous opportunities for the Bible to contain inconsistencies, people who view the Bible with such ideas as 'perfection', 'inerrancy', or 'infallibility' face constant challenges to their faith. The inability to recognize and acknowledge inconsistencies can easily lead to a decreased ability to make the wisest use of the Bible.

The greatest danger is that people who hold the doctrine of Biblical inerrancy may, even unintentionally, come to accept insulting conceptions of the world, mankind, and God. The next few chapters will examine in detail various aspects of the Bible that, when viewed as 'inerrant', are often not adequately appreciated and can therefore contribute to a distorted portrait of God and the Bible.

CHAPTER 5

Pre-scientific Biblical Narratives

One central thesis of this book is that the wisest use of the Bible can be achieved by appreciating the historical context in which it was written. In so doing, one can have less difficulty recognizing and acknowledging inconsistencies and thus be less likely to adopt an inconsistency as absolute truth. Fundamentalists who adhere to a doctrine of inerrancy face a particularly great risk of not being able to recognize implausibilities. One type of implausibility that can be inadequately appreciated by fundamentalists is contained in pre-scientific Biblical narratives. Those narratives often reflect the author's, and his culture's, views of the universe rather than a modern, scientific understanding of the universe. Non-fundamentalists, who are not tied to any doctrines of inerrancy, are free to acknowledge that the Biblical writers displayed what today would be regarded as a crude understanding of science. Non-fundamentalists do not feel that their religious faith is threatened by such an acknowledgment. Yet many fundamentalists, devoted unswervingly to a belief in the total inerrancy of the Bible, would have great difficulty making such an acknowledgment, probably feeling that they, and their faith in God, would be devastated.

The Biblical Picture of the Cosmos

The Biblical view of the universe, for example, which pictured the universe as consisting of three tiers: the heavens, the Earth, and Sheol (the underworld), was a common understanding in Biblical times. Most people perceived the world as it appeared to their senses, supplemented by some seemingly logical, but for the most part inaccurate, speculation.

The world looks flat. It appears to be surrounded by water, which seems also to underlie it. The sky appears to be a blue canopy that covers the earth. Within the canopy are what look like lights (stars), apparently designed to illuminate the Earth. Since water falls from the sky, the blue canopy must contain holes through which the water drops. Although modern science disagrees with that cosmology, those descriptions were common in much of man's earliest cosmological speculation.

Not surprisingly, Biblical authors shared those views. The Earth, which is flat, lies atop a sea (Genesis 7:11; Psalm 136:6). Above the Earth, which is stationary (Psalm 93:1; 104:5), are the heavens, resembling a canopy or an inverted bowl (Genesis 1:6–8; Job 37:18; Isaiah 40:22). Pillars support the circumference of that vault (Job 26:11; Psalm 104:3). The sun, moon, and stars were designed to illuminate the earth for man (Genesis 7:11; Psalm 78:23). Inside the Earth is Sheol, populated by the shadowy dead (Isaiah 14:9–11). The Biblical cosmology differs considerably from the modern cosmology and is scientifically inaccurate.

Contranatural Phenomena

It is the same primitive tendency to describe things as they superficially appear that probably led Biblical authors to describe hares as chewing their cud (Leviticus 11:6). Consider some other examples of narratives that most likely reflect a pre-scientific understanding of the world. Most fundamentalists probably view most, if not all, of the following narratives as literal, accurate accounts of actual historical events. If they view some of them differently—for example, as symbols, allegories, or visions—their reasons for viewing them as such are often due not so much to a critical examination of the narrative as to an overwhelming desire to preserve their doctrine of inerrancy. Whatever may be their views, so long as they tie their faith to treating the Bible as totally free from error, they risk being unable to incorporate into their views a recognition that Biblical writers were sometimes limited in their scientific understanding.

1. The Great Flood of Noah's day covered "all the high mountains under the whole heaven, standing twenty-two feet and more above the highest peaks" (Genesis 7:19–20).

2. "But Lot's wife looked back [at two cities being destroyed] . . . and became a pillar of salt" (Genesis 19:26).

3. Aaron threw down his rod before Pharaoh and his court, "and it became a serpent" (Exodus 7:10). Aaron hit the surface of the Nile with his rod, "and the river turned to blood . . . and there was blood throughout the land of Egypt" (Exodus 7:20–21). Aaron pointed his rod "toward all the rivers, streams, and pools of Egypt," which caused frogs to cover the nation "in every corner of the land" (Exodus 8:5–6). Aaron struck the dust with his rod, and the dust became lice: "and suddenly lice infested the entire nation, covering the Egyptians and their animals" (Exodus 8:16–17). Moses struck a rock with his rod, and "water gushed out" ("enough for everyone" in the wilderness, at least a million people) (Exodus 17:5–6).

4. Moses and Aaron took "ashes from the kiln" and "tossed it toward the sky, and it became boils that broke out on man and animals alike throughout all Egypt" (Exodus 9:10).

5. Moses lifted his hands "to heaven," and "there was thick darkness over all the land for three days. During all that time the people [of Egypt] scarcely moved—but all the people of Israel had light as usual." (Exodus 10:21–23).

6. "The Lord guided them [the Israelites in the wilderness] by a pillar of cloud during the daytime, and by a pillar of fire at night. So they could travel either by day or night. The cloud and fire were never out of sight." (Exodus 13:21–22). "When the Cloud lifted, the people of Israel moved on to wherever it stopped, and camped there. In this way they journeyed at the command of the Lord and stopped where he told them to, then remained there as long as the Cloud stayed." (Numbers 9:17–18). An Angel of God moved a cloud so that it would be between the Egyptians and the people of Israel. Then, "as it changed to a pillar of fire, it gave darkness to the Egyptians but light to the people of Israel!" (Exodus 14:19–20).

7. During the Exodus, according to the Bible, there were over 600,000 Israelite males of military age—not counting women, children, and older men (Numbers 1:17–2:34). This would have made the total Israelite population close to two

million, but Egypt's *entire* population at the time could hardly have been that many.

8. To prove that one's wife has committed adultery, she is brought before the priest to drink "holy water" mixed with "dust from the floor of the Tabernacle": "If she has been defiled, having committed adultery against her husband, the water will become bitter within her, and her body will swell and her thigh will rot. . . . But if she is pure and has not committed adultery, she shall be unharmed and will soon become pregnant." (Numbers 5:17–28).

9. Moses placed twelve wooden rods in the tabernacle, and "when he went in the next day, he found that Aaron's rod, . . . had budded and was blossoming, and had ripe almonds hanging from it!" (Numbers 17:1–8).

10. "And the sun and the moon didn't move until the Israeli army had finished the destruction of its enemies! This is described in greater detail in *The Book of Jashar.* So the sun stopped in the heavens and stayed there for almost twenty-four hours! There had never been such a day before, and there has never been another since, when the Lord stopped the sun and moon—all because of the prayer of one man." (Joshua 10:13–14).

11. Wool placed on the threshing floor one night is wet the next morning ("a whole bowlful of water" is wrung out of it), but the ground is dry. A day or so later, the exact opposite phenomenon occurred: ". . . the fleece stayed dry, but the ground was covered with dew!" (Judges 6:37–40).

12. ". . . Elijah folded his cloak together and struck the water with it; and the river divided and they went across on dry ground!" (2 Kings 2:8). Later that day, Elisha did the same thing, striking the water at the bank of the Jordan River with Elijah's cloak, and "the water parted and Elisha went across!" (2 Kings 2:13–14).

13. As Elijah and Elisha were "walking along, talking, suddenly a chariot of fire, drawn by horses of fire, appeared and drove between them, separating them, and Elijah was carried by a whirlwind to heaven." Elisha cried out that it was "The Chariot of Israel and the charioteers." (2 Kings 2:11–12).

14. ". . . and Elisha cut a stick and threw it into the water; and the axhead [used for "cutting down trees" and "chopping"] rose to the surface and floated" (2 Kings 6:5–7).

15. A dead body was thrown into the tomb of Elisha, and "as soon as the body touched Elisha's bones, the dead man revived and jumped to his feet!" (2 Kings 13:21).

16. When King Hezekiah requested that a miracle be performed by God, Isaiah asked, "Do you want the shadow on the sundial to go forward ten points or backward ten points?" Hezekiah then said, "The shadow always moves forward, . . . [so] make it go backward." And so the Lord "caused the shadow to move ten points backward on the sundial of Ahaz!" (2 Kings 20:8–11).

17. The Bible says that Solomon's Temple was managed by 38,000 servants (1 Chronicles 23:4–5) and cost roughly "several billion dollars worth of gold bullion, millions in silver, and so much iron and bronze that I [David] haven't even weighed it" (1 Chronicles 22:14). Yet the edifice was only "ninety feet long, thirty feet wide, and forty-five feet high" (1 Kings 6:2). And there is no archaeological or historical evidence (excluding the Bible) of the existence of Solomon's Temple, even though this extraordinary temple would have been located only a few miles from well-travelled trade routes.

18. A leper said to Jesus, "Sir, if you want to, you can heal me." Then Jesus touched the man, said "I want to," and commanded, "Be healed." Then, the leprosy disappeared "instantly". (Matthew 8:2–3). Jesus told a man with a deformed hand, "Reach out your hand." The man did so, "and instantly his hand was healed!" (Mark 3:1–5).

19. Jesus "took five loaves of bread and two fish, looked up into the sky and asked God's blessing on the meal, then broke the loaves apart and gave them to the disciples to place before the people. And everyone ate until full! And when the scraps were picked up afterwards, there were twelve basketfuls left over! (About 5,000 men were in the crowd that day, besides all the women and children.)" (Matthew 14:16–21). On another occasion, Jesus gave seven loaves of bread and "a few small fish" to a crowd, "And everyone ate until

full—4,000 men besides the women and children! And afterwards, when the scraps were picked up, there were seven basketfuls left over!" (Matthew 15:32–38).

20. "[A boy] can't talk because he is possessed by a demon. And whenever the demon is in control of him it dashes him to the ground and makes him foam at the mouth and grind his teeth and become rigid. . . . When Jesus saw the crowd was growing he rebuked the demon. 'O demon of deafness and dumbness,' he said, 'I command you to come out of this child. . . .' Then the demon screamed terribly and convulsed the boy again and left him;. . ." (Mark 9:17–26).

21. Jesus told his disciples that if "those who believe . . . drink anything poisonous, it won't hurt them" (Mark 16:18).

22. After Jesus died, "tombs opened, and many godly men and women who had died came back to life again. After Jesus' resurrection, they left the cemetery and went into Jerusalem, and appeared to many people there." (Matthew 27:52–53). Yet Mark's, Luke's, and John's Gospels fail to mention the seemingly unforgettable and significant occurrence, and no historical sources have been found to document it.

THE BIBLE AND THE THEORY OF EVOLUTION

One area of thought in which many fundamentalists feel obliged to contradict modern scientific theory is illustrated in the debate between evolutionism and creationism.

"Scientific evolution eliminates belief in God or special creation." That statement reflects the precarious position in which many fundamentalists place their faith when they try to tie it to an understanding of the Bible that requires it to be the final (and complete) word. The statement comes from Pat Robertson (page 61 in his book *Answers to 200 of Life's Most Probing Questions*). Mr. Robertson's views on evolution represent those of many fundamentalists, who regard the book of Genesis as expressing a definitive history of human origin. Accordingly, Mr. Robertson writes: "These original humans [Adam and Eve] were not subhuman or Neanderthal creatures. They were beautiful human beings created in the image of God, with tremendous intelligence and ability. If man has gone away from that, he has gone down instead of up" (p. 55).

For the reasons just cited, many fundamentalists are predisposed to reject evolutionary theory. That predisposition makes them more likely than they would otherwise be to accept even the weakest anti-evolutionary arguments. Perhaps the weakest anti-evolutionary argument goes as follows: Although evolutionary theory is just that, 'simply a theory', belief in the creation story of Genesis is based on Divine revelation and hence more credible than 'mere theory'. Accordingly, Pat Robertson writes: "The ascending order of living creatures is an observable fact. Apart from the Bible or the revelation of God, the source of their origin is unknown and scientific speculation about their origin can only be theory—never fact" (p. 61).

That argument trades on a misunderstanding of the expression 'scientific theory'. Scientific theories are attempts to provide explanations that are supposed to be presented in accordance with the scientific method. Typically, scientific theories are judged on the degree to which they can explain present, past, and future phenomena. In choosing one scientific theory over another, the relative amount of evidence in support of each theory must be determined. In contrast, the strength with which a belief is held does not, in and of itself, elevate a theory into a law. For many people have held with unswerving conviction beliefs that have turned out to be false. Creationism, even though it is based on a firm belief in the Bible, is therefore as much a *theory* of the origin of species as is evolution.

Another particularly weak argument that some fundamentalists accept is that disagreements about evolution are so widespread among scientists that the theory is about to be discarded. That argument stems from a failure to appreciate the distinction between the theory of evolution and that of natural selection. The theory of evolution, accepted by nearly all biologists, holds that organisms have gradually changed over millions of years. That theory has been accepted by many thinkers for thousands of years. The theory of evolution is not the source of substantial disagreement among most scientists.

Rather, disagreement revolves around the mechanisms by which evolution occurs. The theory of natural selection,

proposed by Darwin only a century ago, specifies one particular mechanism. According to the theory, only those organisms that can adapt to their environments will survive and
reproduce in the 'struggle for existence'. While there is some
disagreement among scientists about whether natural selection is the only mechanism for evolution, most scientists accept natural selection as at least a partial explanation for how
evolution occurs. Disagreements among scientists are essen-
tial to scientific progress; they are necessary to evaluate the
relative strength of scientific theories.

Many people do not realize that natural selection has
been observed: for example, after years of exposure to particular poisons, mosquitoes and rats have become resistant to
them. Furthermore, selective breeding has enabled human
beings to develop racehorses, hunting dogs, homing pigeons,
and so on. While human breeders have deliberately effected
significant changes in animals by breeding only those animals with certain traits considered desirable, Darwin maintained that nature effects such biological changes
automatically.

Many fundamentalists acknowledge that gradual
changes have occurred over time within certain biological divisions, but they maintain that there are barriers against further change. Accordingly, Pat Robertson writes:

> [O]ne major empirical fact negates the theory of scientific evolution.
> There has never been one observable case of any creature shifting (or
> evolving) from one biological class to another or from one phylum to
> another. There is no case where we have remains or fossils of an ani-
> mal that died during the evolutionary process. The reason is clear. The
> Bible says that God made each animal 'after its kind' through a special
> act of creation for each of them.
>   I think the greatest example of this truth is the mule. The mule is a
> cross between a donkey and a horse. Mules are born sterile. They are
> unable to reproduce themselves. In other words, the horse and the
> donkey were close enough in the biological ladder to interbreed with
> each other, but their offspring could not continue the breeding proc-
> ess. Even that close link could not reproduce. Certainly nobody has
> ever bred a bird with a snake or an ape with a man. There is no repro-
> ductive evidence to support it. (p. 61)

It is, however, unjustified to maintain with certainty that
modern understanding of evolution is incompatible with re-

productive evidence. Since human beings have been breeding plants and animals for only a few thousand years, one cannot be sure about the limits of breeding if conducted for millions of years. Further, fossils often show gradual changes over millions of years, and show evidence of species of extinct animals (such as the pterodactyl) incapable of adapting to their environments.

Many fundamentalists feel obliged to reject modern understandings of evolution and natural selection because they believe that those scientific explanations are incompatible with Divine purpose, and that they appeal only to random forces. Accordingly, Pat Robertson writes:

> The Bible does not teach random evolution. The Bible does teach an act of creation by God of a universe out of a formless void, and then individual acts of creation in an ascending order from the simpler forms of aquatic life to the mammals and finally to a creature made in God's image—man. Human beings did not evolve out of the primordial ooze. They are the special creation of an all-powerful God.
>
> Therefore, it can be said that the Bible teaches 'creation in ascending order.' When the scientists discover the ascending order of the plants and animals on earth, their factual observations are generally in harmony with the Bible. The scientists go wrong, however, when they attempt to draw theological theories of origins from their findings. (p. 61)

When Pat Robertson holds that the Bible does not teach evolution, suggests that Biblical teaching is opposed to evolution, and holds that scientific theories of evolution postulate 'random' factors, he appears to be holding that scientific explanation *precludes* the possibility of theological reflection about cosmic design and purpose. He appears to be saying that, if reference to God is not part of every explanation (including scientific explanation) of human origin and development, then human beings must be considered the products of 'random' forces.

That belief is subject to the following two objections. First, to the scientist, the principles cited in evolutionary theories are not entirely random but quite orderly; indeed, governed by scientific law. Second, the professional concerns of scientists do not touch on cosmic design, though the principles and mechanisms behind evolution could be part of some cosmic design. Scientists are not necessarily unreligious; rather, as scientists, they are concerned with using the scientific method to understand how natural phenomena are connected in law-like relations to other natural phenomena. Accordingly, scientists have attempted to understand the origin and development of human beings by appealing to such mechanisms as natural selection. The scientist, then, leaves to the theologian and the philosopher whether those natural phenomena are part of a cosmic plan.

While many fundamentalists feel obliged to reject scientific theories because of their belief in the scientific inerrancy of the Biblical authors, non-fundamentalists can at least entertain the possibility both that the authors were at times scientifically mistaken and that God might operate through principles of evolution and natural selection.

CONCLUSION

The reader has seen how a pre-scientific understanding led to Biblical implausibilities. As will be seen in the next chapter, given a pre-scientific understanding and the natural human tendency to describe the world in anthropomorphic terms, the Biblical writers perceived many of their tragedies and successes, as well as their ethical views, as reflecting God's will. And sometimes, as will be illustrated, that viewpoint led to ascribing morally dubious actions to God. Yet fundamentalists who generally perceive the Bible only as 'inerrant', may be risking their ability to make such moral distinctions, ultimately a serious hazard to their faith.

CHAPTER 6

THE POSSIBILITY OF MORAL PROGRESS

Many fundamentalists risk picturing God as a tyrant when they require certain Biblical verses to be literally free from error. Although the Biblical depiction of God generally is progressively humane, many Biblical verses, particularly those of early origin, insultingly depict Him as cruel and unjust. That fact need not alarm even the most devout non-fundamentalists, who can easily accept the notion that Biblical theology and morality show a fairly steady (though of course not absolute) progress. With the ability to recognize that source of potential Biblical inconsistencies, such non-fundamentalists will most likely *not* come to believe that God is cruel, unjust, or tyrannical.

A POSSIBLE MORAL PROGRESS SCENARIO

In the earliest parts of the Bible, Yahweh (the God of the Old Testament) is depicted as capricious, as when He met Moses at an inn and tried to kill him, only to be stopped by the circumcision of Moses' son (Exodus 4:24–26). Yahweh was also pictured as endorsing the punishment of innocent people for the sins of the guilty, as when Achan's entire family was put to death because *he* secreted booty from Jericho (Joshua 7), or when Saul's two sons and five grandsons were killed because *Saul* slaughtered the Gibeonites (2 Samuel 21:1–9).

Although those examples are considered today flagrant violations of people's rights, they reflect the ancient view of corporate responsibility, in which it was considered right to punish people for the sins of their family or tribe. Similarly, animal sacrifice reflected the ancient belief that the shedding of blood could purge people of their sins. As the Hebrews developed, they rejected the dubious use of corporate responsibility (Deuteronomy 24:16), and began to subordinate the practice of animal sacrifice to the value of social justice (Micah 6:6–8).

Nearly all non-fundamentalists can admit—and thus strengthen, not weaken, their faith—that at least some of the morality endorsed in the earliest parts of the Bible is clearly inferior to much of the morality reflected both in the later prophets of the Old Testament and in many of the teachings of Jesus and Paul. (That is not to say that moral codes may not also *regress* at times but only that they do change with time. Indeed, although the claim of clear and consistent moral progress in the Bible is a subject of controversy, the fact that Biblical injunctions are at times products of diverse moral codes is evident.)

Many fundamentalists, however, may often have trouble accounting for the notion of *any* Biblical moral progress because they believe that the Biblical writers inerrantly recorded all the actions and commands of God. To recognize any elements of moral progress requires recognizing some morally dubious actions and practices endorsed in the Bible. While most non-fundamentalists are free to do that, fundamentalists face the potentially serious hazard of being unable to recognize and acknowledge any moral changes reflected in the Bible. For to do so requires acknowledging the likelihood that the Hebrew view of God and morality was conditioned by human limitations. Sometimes the Hebrew authors may have ascribed to God actions and practices that were in *their* best interests but might not necessarily have been just. Thus, for example, the author could explain a military defeat of the Hebrews as *God's* punishment for disobedience.

Consider then, in this chapter, some examples of the atrocities, injustices, and general barbarism that were described as being demanded, endorsed, or committed by the God of the Old Testament. All these are examples that fundamentalists may risk feeling impelled to defend as morally right, rather than to appreciate them more fully as reflecting the Biblical authors' limited points of view.

INJUSTICE IN THE BIBLE

Two central moral principles of justice are that only the guilty should be punished, and that the punishment should fit the crime. Indeed, according to the Bible, God said: "Fathers shall not be put to death for the sins of their sons nor the sons for the sins of their fathers; every man worthy of death shall be executed for his own crime" (Deuteronomy 24:16). Yet the Old Testament has God often assigning the death penalty for fairly harmless actions and causing the innocent to suffer for the sins of the guilty.

When God issued His Ten Commandments, He reportedly proclaimed that "when I punish people for their sins, the punishment continues upon the children, grandchildren, and great-grandchildren of those who hate me" (Exodus 20:5).

In 2 Samuel, the Bible records, with no apparent explanation, that "Once again the anger of the Lord flared against Israel" (24:1). He then "caused David to harm them by taking a national census." After the census was taken, Yahweh is described as having informed David that he had three choices of how he would be punished for having taken the census: "Seven years of famine across the land," "three months before your enemies," or "three days of plague" (24:13). David chose the pestilence as the least of the evils. In three days, 70,000 innocent Hebrews died. Horrified and puzzled, David was moved to cry out: "Look, I am the one who has sinned! What have these sheep done? Let your anger be only against me and my family" (24:17).

God is described as having administered excessive and misplaced punishment to the Israelites when they were in the desert. The Bible says that Korah had "conspired with Dathan and Abiram . . . to incite a rebellion against Moses." Two hundred and fifty members of the Assembly were "involved" in the rebellion. The Bible gives no indication that any acts of violence were committed by them, but Korah did question Moses' authority to govern. As a result, Yahweh, according to the Bible, told Moses and Aaron, "Get away from these people so that I may instantly destroy them." The Bible then says that Moses and Aaron "pleaded" with God, asking, ". . . must you be angry with all the people when one man sins?" Despite the pleading "a great fissure swallowed them [the 250 people] up, along with their tents and families and the friends who were standing with them . . . and they perished." Later, the Bible says, "all the people began muttering again against

Moses and Aaron saying, 'You have killed the Lord's people.'"
For that sentiment, the Lord is described as having sent a
plague that killed 14,700 people. Indeed, had Aaron not
rushed in with a censer of incense to make an atonement for
his people, the plague presumably would have eventually
killed everyone. (Numbers 16.)

FREQUENT DEATH PENALTIES

At times, the Old Testament can reverently be questioned in
the light of the moral principle that the punishment must fit
the crime. With that thought in mind consider that Yahweh is
described as having commanded the death penalty for a
number of offenses:

> If a man marries a girl, then after sleeping with her accuses her of hav-
> ing had premarital intercourse with another man, . . . [and] if the
> man's accusations are true, . . . the judges shall take the girl to the door
> of her father's home where the men of the city shall stone her to death.
> She has defiled Israel by flagrant crime, being a prostitute while living
> at home with her parents; and such evil must be cleansed from among
> you. (Deuteronomy 22:13–21)

The death penalty just stated was imposed *only* on women.

> If a man commits adultery with another man's wife, both the man and
> woman shall be put to death. (Leviticus 20:10)

Yet, "If a man seduces a slave girl who is engaged to be married, they shall be tried in a court but not put to death." The
reason for not executing them: "she is not free". (Leviticus
19:20)

> A sorceress must be put to death (Exodus 22:18)

That verse inspired the executions of hundreds of thousands,
if not millions, of women, particularly between the 1480s and
the 1700s.

> A medium or a wizard—whether man or woman—shall surely be
> stoned to death. (Leviticus 20:27)

Further, while many of the laws ascribed to God were especially intended for His own people, He is pictured as having punished those who would, in any way, speak against
Him, whether Hebrew or non-Hebrew:

Out in the camp one day, a young man whose mother was an Israelite and whose father was an Egyptian, got into a fight with one of the men of Israel. During the fight the Egyptian man's son cursed God,. . .

And the Lord said to Moses, "Take him outside the camp and tell all who heard him to lay their hands upon his head; then all the people are to execute him by stoning. And tell the people of Israel that anyone who curses his God must pay the penalty: he must die. All the congregation shall stone him; this law applies to the foreigner as well as to the Israelite who blasphemes the name of Jehovah. He must die. . . ."

So they took the youth out of the camp and stoned him until he died, as Jehovah had commanded Moses. (Leviticus 24:10–23)

Death Penalties for Prohibited Worship and Ceremonial Irregularities

The Biblical God's punishment for not properly worshipping Him or for not believing in Him also can be perceived as excessive. He is described as having boasted of His jealousy and having promised to punish both the people who broke His laws and the descendants of those people:

> You shall not bow down to any images nor worship them in any way, for I am the Lord your God. I am a jealous God, and I will bring the curse of a father's sins upon even the third and fourth generation of the children of those who hate me;. . . (Deuteronomy 5:9; similarly, Exodus 20:5; 34:6–7, 14)

When God first spoke to Moses at Mount Sinai, He is described as having instructed Moses to "Set boundary lines the people may not pass, and tell them, 'Beware! Do not go up into the mountain, or even touch its boundaries; whoever does shall die'" (Exodus 19:12). According to the Bible, He also told Moses to tell the people that "no hand shall touch him [God], but he shall be stoned or shot to death with arrows, whether man or animal" (Exodus 19:13).

God is claimed to have commanded that people kill members of their family who worship other Gods:

> If your nearest relative or closest friend, even a brother, son, daughter, or beloved wife whispers to you to come and worship these foreign gods, do not consent nor listen, and have no pity: do not spare that person from the penalty; don't conceal his horrible suggestion. Execute him! Your own hand shall be the first upon him to put him to death, then the hands of all the people. Stone him to death because he

has tried to draw you away from the Lord your God who brought you from the land of Egypt, the place of slavery. (Deuteronomy 13:6–10)

He is also represented as having commanded death for violating the Sabbath:

Yes, rest on the Sabbath, for it is holy. Anyone who does not obey this command must die; anyone who does any work on that day shall be killed. (Exodus 31:14–15)

Accordingly, when a man in the wilderness was caught "gathering wood on the Sabbath day," the "Lord" reportedly said: "The man must die—all the people shall stone him to death outside the camp" (Numbers 15:32–36).

The "Lord" instructed Aaron, "Never drink wine or strong drink when you go into the Tabernacle, lest you die" (Leviticus 10:8–9). And the "Lord" told Moses, "They must always wash before doing so [going into the Tabernacle], or they will die" (Exodus 30:20). The "Lord" killed seventy of the men of Beth-Shemesh who were offering sacrifices to the Lord "because they [had] looked into the Ark" (1 Samuel 6:19).

The Bible records that when Aaron's sons, Nadab and Abihu, "placed unholy fire in their censers, laid incense on the fire, and offered the incense before the Lord—contrary to what the Lord had just commanded them," a "fire blazed forth from the presence of the Lord and destroyed them" (Leviticus 10:1–2). No indication is given that the sons had made a deliberate mistake or were intoxicated; they were apparently just careless. Moses explained to Aaron: "This is what the Lord meant when he said, 'I will show myself holy among those who approach me, and I will be glorified before all the people'" (10:3). Moses then cautioned Aaron and his other sons that if they showed any signs of mourning, "God will strike you dead too, and his wrath will come upon all the people of Israel" (10:6).

At least one time, the "Lord" is represented as having requested indiscriminate slaughter in order that His people might "ordain" themselves:

[Moses] told them, "Jehovah the God of Israel says, 'Get your swords and go back and forth from one end of the camp to the other and kill even your brothers, friends, and neighbors.'" So they did, and about three thousand men died that day. Then Moses told the Levites, "Today you have ordained yourselves for the service of the Lord, for you obeyed him even though it meant killing your own sons and brothers; now he will give you a great blessing." (Exodus 32:27–29)

On another occasion, the Bible records:

... the Lord instructed one of the prophets to say to another man, "Strike me with your sword!" But the man refused. Then the prophet told him, "Because you have not obeyed the voice of the Lord, a lion shall kill you as soon as you leave me." And sure enough, as he turned to go a lion attacked and killed him. (1 Kings 20:35–36)

Joshua told the people that God's demands of His subjects are exacting, and that the cost of any disobedience would be great:

... be very sure to follow all the instructions written in the book of the laws of Moses; do not deviate from them the least little bit; ... do not even mention the names of their [the heathens'] gods, much less swear by them or worship them. . . . But as certainly as the Lord has given you the good things he promised, just as certainly he will bring evil upon you if you disobey him. For if you worship other gods he will completely wipe you out from this good land. . . . His anger will rise hot against you, and you will quickly perish." (Joshua 23:6, 7, 15, 16)

SLAUGHTERING OF DISOBEDIENT HEBREWS

Yahweh was pictured as sometimes less than merciful in dealing with His chosen people, the Hebrews, when any of them disobeyed Him. He is even claimed to have feared that He might be tempted to destroy them on their journey to the Promised Land: "I will not travel among you, for you are a stubborn, unruly people, and I would be tempted to destroy you along the way" (Exodus 33:3).

When the Hebrews expressed their wish to return to Egypt after being told by spies that the Canaanites were giants, Yahweh, according to the Bible, gave the following instructions to Moses and Aaron:

Tell them, "The Lord vows to do to you what you feared: You will all die here in the wilderness! Not a single one of you twenty years old and older, who has complained against me, shall enter the Promised Land. . . . You must wander in the desert like nomads for forty years. In this way you will pay for your faithlessness, until the last of you lies dead in the desert." (Numbers 14:32–33)

When the Hebrews "began to murmur against God and to complain against Moses," asking "Why have you brought us out of Egypt to die here in the wilderness?" and saying "There is nothing to eat here, and nothing to drink, and we hate this insipid manna", the Lord "sent poisonous snakes among them, . . . and many of them were bitten and died" (Numbers 21:5–6).

In Hosea, the Biblical God told rebellious Samaria that she "must bear the guilt," and "will be killed by the invading army, her babies dashed to death against the ground, her pregnant women ripped open with a sword" (Hosea 13:16).

SLAUGHTERING OF CHILDREN

Sometimes Yahweh was pictured as having endorsed or condoned excessively harsh treatment of children. For example, Yahweh is described as having administered swift punishment when some children poked fun at the bald-headed prophet Elisha:

> As he [Elisha] was walking along the road, a gang of young men from the city began mocking and making fun of him because of his bald head. He turned around and cursed them in the name of the Lord; and two female bears came out of the woods and tore forty-two of them. (2 Kings 2:23–24)

(The phrase translated "a gang of young men" is most often translated as "children". See our discussion of this passage in Chapter 8, where we investigate the importance of alternative translations of Scripture.)

The story of Jephthah, while illustrating the danger of thoughtless vows, may also be seen as another example of the mistreatment of children. Before going into battle with the Ammonites, Jephthah vowed that if he defeated them, he would sacrifice to the Lord whoever walked from his house to meet him (Judges 11:31). After he returned home in triumph, he encountered a horrible surprise:

> When Jephthah returned home his daughter—his only child—ran out to meet him, playing on a tambourine and dancing for joy. When he saw her he tore his clothes in anguish. . . . And she said, "Father, you must do whatever you promised the Lord, for he has given you a great victory over your enemies,. . ." (Judges 11:34–36)

Two months later, Jephthah carried out his vow to the Lord (Judges 11:39).

Indeed, the mistreatment of children is sometimes endorsed in the Bible. Yahweh is represented as having demanded the execution of those who cursed their parents and the stoning to death (without trial) of incorrigible children:

> Anyone who curses his father or mother shall surely be put to death. . . . (Leviticus 20:9)

> If a man has a stubborn, rebellious son who will not obey his father or mother, even though they punish him, then his father and mother shall take him before the elders of the city and declare, "This son of ours is stubborn and rebellious and won't obey; he is a worthless drunkard." Then the men of the city shall stone him to death. (Deuteronomy 21:18–21)

SLAUGHTERING OF GENTILES—MEN, WOMEN, AND CHILDREN

"O Babylon, evil beast, you shall be destroyed. Blessed is the man who takes your babies and smashes them against the rocks." (Psalm 137:9) The psalmist's remark about his enemies is consistent with the mistreatment of non-Hebrews elsewhere pictured as having been endorsed by the Biblical God. Such endorsements were particularly common when the Bible portrayed God as seeking to fulfill a promise of conquest. In Deuteronomy 7:16, for example, the Biblical God tells the Hebrews, "You must destroy all the nations which the Lord your God delivers into your hands. Have no pity, and do not worship their gods. . . ."

In Numbers 31, Moses, according to the Bible, was ordered by Yahweh to attack the Midianites. After the Hebrew army killed almost all the Midianites, burned down their cities, and brought back all the women and children, Moses learned, to his dismay, that the women had been spared:

> "Why have you let all the women live?" he demanded. "These are the very ones who followed Balaam's advice and caused the people of Israel to worship idols on Mount Peor, and they are the cause of the plague [promised by God] that destroyed us. Now kill all the boys and all the women who have had sexual intercourse. Only the little girls may live; you may keep them for yourselves." (31:15–18)

The total of "32,000 young girls" was thus apportioned among the army and the people; thirty-two of the girls were given to the Levites (31:35, 40).

In Deuteronomy 7:1–2, when Yahweh is described as having promised that He would destroy the Hittites, the Girgashites, the Amorites, the Canaanites, the Perizzites, the Hivites, and the Jebusites, Moses told the Hebrews:

> When the Lord your God delivers them over to you to be destroyed, do a complete job of it—don't make any treaties or show them mercy; utterly wipe them out. (Deuteronomy 7:2)

The book of Joshua provides some examples of how it was thought that Yahweh had fulfilled His promise. It is claimed that He told Joshua, the new leader of the Hebrews after Moses's death, that His people "shall conquer all the land I promised to their ancestors" (1:6). Joshua's military conquests began with the fall of Jericho, where, according to the Bible, God had told Joshua to kill everyone except those living in Rahab's house. Thus, ". . . the walls of Jericho crumbled and fell before them" (6:20). "They destroyed everything in it—men and women, young and old; oxen; sheep; donkeys—everything" (6:21). Afterwards, God is claimed to have instructed Joshua to "take the entire army and go to Ai, for it is now yours to conquer. . . . You shall do to them as you did to Jericho and her King; but this time you may keep the loot and the cattle for yourselves." (8:1, 2) Accordingly, the Bible says, "When the army of Israel had finished slaughtering all the men outside the city, they went back and finished off everyone left inside. So the entire population of Ai, twelve thousand in all, was wiped out that day." (8:24–25)

Indeed, throughout the book of Joshua, many of the Biblical God's efforts to fulfill His promise of the "land of milk and honey" for His chosen people are recorded. All the following verse groupings in Joshua contain distinct statements indicating that the entire populations of particular cities and regions were annihilated under the supposedly express orders and approval of the Biblical God: 6:17, 21; 8:2, 24–25; 10:29–30; 10:31–32; 10:34–35; 10:36–37; 10:38–39; 10:40–43; 11:10–11; 11:12; 11:16–20; and 11:21, 22.

The Bible also reveals a result of this destruction of the "enemies":

> So in this way the Lord gave to Israel all the land he had promised to their ancestors, and they went in and conquered it and lived there. And the Lord gave them peace, just as he had promised, and no one could stand against them; the Lord helped them destroy all their enemies. (Joshua 21:43, 44)

GOD'S ALLEGED USE OF DECEPTION

Sometimes God is pictured as having used deceptive tactics to destroy those who stood in the way of His chosen people. For example, in several of Joshua's conquests, God is represented as having made certain that the opponent would not choose to make a peace treaty rather than to be destroyed in war: "For the Lord made the enemy kings want to fight the Israelis [sic] instead of asking for peace; so they were mercilessly killed, as the Lord had commanded Moses" (Joshua 11:20).

The book of Exodus reveals Yahweh's deceptive plans for gaining His people's freedom from Egyptian bondage. Yahweh is claimed to have told Moses:

> When you arrive back in Egypt you are to go to Pharaoh and do the miracles I have shown you, but I will make him stubborn so that he will not let the people go. Then you are to tell him, "Jehovah says, 'Israel is my eldest son, and I have commanded you to let him go away and worship me, but you have refused; and now see, I will slay your eldest son.'" (4:21–22)

Thus, Moses told Pharaoh that Yahweh demanded him to "Let my people go" (5:1). According to the Bible, as a result of God's hardening Pharaoh's heart, Pharaoh intensified the Israelites' suffering. Moses now "protested" to God:

> Lord, . . . how can you mistreat your own people like this? Why did you ever send me, if you were going to do this to them? Ever since I gave Pharaoh your message, he has only been more and more brutal to them, and you have not delivered them at all! (5:22–23)

God is claimed to have replied:

> Tell Aaron everything I say to you, and he will announce it to Pharaoh, demanding that the people of Israel be allowed to leave Egypt. But I will cause Pharaoh to stubbornly refuse, and I will multiply my miracles in Egypt. Yet even then Pharaoh won't listen to you; so I will crush Egypt with a final disaster and then lead my people out. (7:2–4)

What followed was a series of miraculous plagues. Yet after each one Pharaoh remained stubborn because, according to the Biblical description of God's plan, He did not intend for Pharaoh to let the people go until Egypt was made to suffer great disaster. Indeed, even after all the men in the fields were killed by one of the plagues, Pharaoh stubbornly refused to let the people go.

God is then claimed to have told Moses:

> Go back again and make your demand upon Pharaoh; but I have hardened him and his officials, so that I can do more miracles demonstrating my powers. What stories you can tell your children and grandchildren about the incredible things I am doing in Egypt! (10:1–2)

Another plague followed, and the Bible says again, "the Lord hardened Pharaoh's heart and he would not let them go" (10:27). Now God reportedly sent the final disaster: Yahweh killed all the firstborn sons in the land of Egypt (12:29), passing over only the people of Israel. The Bible says that, "Then Pharaoh and his officials and all the people of Egypt got up in the night; and there was bitter crying throughout all the land of Egypt, for there was not a house where there was not one dead" (12:30). Now, finally, Pharaoh let the people go.

But that was not the last plan that God is said to have had for Pharaoh and the Egyptians. When the people of Israel left Egypt, the Lord, according to the Bible, told Moses, "I will harden the hearts of the Egyptians and they will go in after you and you will see the honor I will get in defeating Pharaoh and all his armies, chariots, and horsemen" (14:17). So when the Lord opened up a path through the sea for His people, the Egyptians followed. And then Moses stretched out his hand as God reportedly had directed him to do, and the Bible records what happened:

> The Egyptians tried to flee, but the Lord drowned them in the sea. The water covered the path and the chariots and horsemen. And of all the army of Pharaoh that chased after Israel through the sea, not one remained alive. (14:27–28)

In 1 Kings, Yahweh is also described as having countenanced deception in His effort to destroy King Ahab of Israel, who was "especially guilty because he worshipped idols" (21:26). According to the prophet Micaiah, the Lord planned to encourage Ahab to go into a losing battle. Ahab's 400 heathen prophets had all assured the king that God would help him to conquer the city of Ramoth-gilead. When Ahab then asked Micaiah, a prophet of God, "shall we attack Ramoth-gilead, or not?" Micaiah replied, "Why, of course! Go right ahead! You will have a great victory, for the Lord will cause you to conquer!" (22:15) But soon Micaiah admitted what he believed was the true plan of his Lord:

> Listen to this further word from the Lord. I saw the Lord sitting on his throne, and the armies of heaven stood around him. Then the Lord said, "Who will entice Ahab to go and die at Ramoth-gilead?" Various suggestions were made, until one angel approached the Lord and said, "I'll do it!" "How," the Lord asked. And he replied, "I will go as a lying spirit in the mouths of all his prophets." And the Lord said, "That will do it; you will succeed. Go ahead." (22:19–22)

Micaiah concluded, "Don't you see? The Lord has put a lying spirit in the mouths of all these prophets, but the fact of the matter is that the Lord has decreed disaster upon you" (22:23). Although Micaiah had admitted the truth, Ahab accepted his lying prophets' advice. Thus, as the Biblical God had planned, Ahab was killed in the battle at Ramoth-gilead (22:35–37).

In 2 Kings, however, God is portrayed as still desiring vengeance, establishing Jehu as a puppet-ruler to exterminate all remnants of Ahab's dynasty:

> So Jehu left the others and went into the house, and the young man [Elisha's prophet] poured the oil over his head and said, "The Lord God of Israel says, 'I anoint you king of the Lord's people, Israel. You are to destroy the family of Ahab; you will avenge the murder of my prophets [apparently killed before Ahab's rule] and of all my other people who were killed by Jezebel [Ahab's wife]. The entire family of Ahab must be wiped out—every male, no matter who. I will destroy the family of Ahab as I destroyed the families of Jeroboam (son of Nebat) and of Baasha (son of Ahijah).'" (9:6–9)

Later, obeying Jehu's further instructions, all seventy of Ahab's sons were murdered: ". . . and their heads were packed into baskets and presented to Jehu at Jezreel. . . ." (10:7). Then, says the Bible:

> Jehu . . . killed all the rest of the members of the family of Ahab who were in Jezreel, as well as all of his important officials, personal friends, and private chaplains. Finally, no one was left who had been close to him in any way. (10:11)

After that, Jehu met the brothers of King Ahaziah of Judah:

> "Grab them!" Jehu shouted to his men. And he took them out to the cistern and killed all forty-two of them. (10:14)

And then he killed all the worshippers of Baal:

> As the priests of Baal began offering sacrifices and burnt offerings, Jehu surrounded the building with eighty of his men. . . . So they slaughtered them all and dragged their bodies outside. . . . (10:24–25)

Yet after all this killing, the Bible portrays the Lord as pleased:

> Afterwards the Lord said to Jehu, "You have done well in following my instructions to destroy the dynasty of Ahab. Because of this I will cause your son, grandson, and your great-grandson to be the Kings of Israel." (10:30)

CONCLUSION

While many non-fundamentalist Christians can acknowledge that the Hebrews would at times ascribe to God their own morally dubious actions and practices, fundamentalists may come dangerously close to believing that all such Biblical descriptions are literally accurate. As will be seen in the next chapter, just as non-fundamentalists are free to acknowledge that the Biblical portrait of God can easily be viewed as sometimes falling short of the ideal of a good God, they may also be in a better position than fundamentalists to appreciate a more balanced view of the Biblical depiction of Jesus.

CHAPTER 7

A BALANCED VIEW OF THE BIBLICAL JESUS

Most non-fundamentalists can acknowledge, with relative ease, that Biblical verses may exist that portray Jesus' character and teachings as sometimes less than perfectly wise. They can recognize that Jesus might have, for example, been subject to some of the cultural prejudices of his day. That recognition need not in any way threaten their faith or preclude them from putting to good use even verses that portray Jesus as having limitations. For example, the Biblical Jesus' invective against the Pharisees (Matthew 23:17) can be viewed as underscoring the importance of avoiding hypocrisy.

Most fundamentalists, however, risk being unable to achieve such a balanced view of the Biblical Jesus when they require the entire Bible to contain information and portraits of Divinity that are always consistent with absolute truth. They can interpret the Bible as always portraying Jesus as perfect, but they may be unable to perceive the Bible as ever portraying Jesus as imperfect. Accordingly, whenever the Bible may present Jesus as making a mistake, fundamentalists may be liable to view such a portrayal not as reflecting some imperfection but rather as defining another part of their concept of perfection.

The ultimate hazards of viewing some imperfections as actually part of one's definition of perfection are obvious. Consider some of the verses that even faithful Christians have recognized as suggesting that Jesus sometimes exhibited less-than-perfect wisdom, or that his life and teachings may not always be inerrantly represented in the Bible, or both possibilities. Try to understand how a fundamentalist approach to the Bible as inerrant may invite difficulties, making it difficult to appreciate fully these verses and ultimately hampering one's ability to attain the fullest possible understanding of Jesus Christ.

THE CHARACTER OF JESUS

Although Jesus, as depicted in the Bible, obviously possessed a number of admirable traits, including compassion, fairness, generosity, sensitivity, and lovingkindness, he seems to be portrayed in the Bible at times as narrow-minded, vindictive, discourteous, ethnocentric, and even hypocritical. The Bible sometimes paints Jesus in what appears to be a less than flattering light and to represent him as having some moral defects. It is difficult if not impossible to reconcile this interpretation of Jesus' conduct with the standards that the Biblical Jesus acknowledged necessary for a perfect servant of God.

While the Biblical Jesus commanded people to love their enemies, to pray for their persecutors (Matthew 5:44), and never to demean others by angrily calling them hurtful names, such as "idiot" (Matthew 5:22), he is represented sometimes as having given vent to a vindictive fury in which he called people "vipers" and "fools". Consider his remarks to people whom he regarded as hypocritical:

> You brood of snakes! How could evil men like you speak what is good and right? (Matthew 12:34)

> Snakes! Sons of vipers! How shall you escape the judgement of Hell? (Matthew 23:33)

> [To the Pharisees he shouted:] Blind fools! (Matthew 23:17)

It is hypocritical for people to condemn others for vindictive name-calling while they substitute invective and vituperation for attempts at dialogue. People rarely if ever profit from ridicule, and angry name-calling rarely if ever heals people. It appears to be hypocritical for the Biblical Jesus to have called even the hypocritical Pharisees "blind fools".

Although the Biblical Jesus commanded people to love everyone impartially and to love and pray for their enemies (Matthew 5:45), the Bible implies that he sometimes did not live up to those standards, or to the standards endorsed by Paul, who commanded people to feed their hungry enemies without hesitation (Romans 12:20). Consider the following example. When a Canaanite woman pleaded with the Biblical Jesus to exorcise her daughter, who was probably in great pain, he at first hesitated to help and answered, "I was sent to help the Jews—the lost sheep of Israel—not the Gentiles" (Matthew 15:24). Even after the woman fell to her feet and begged him to help her daughter, the Biblical Jesus said, "It doesn't seem right to take bread from the children and throw it to the dogs" (Matthew 15:26). Note that most Jews in Jesus' day thought ill of dogs, and that "dogs" in the context of the present story very likely refers to *non-Jews*. Note further that it was only when the woman abased herself by saying that even "puppies" ("dogs" in both the *King James* and *Revised Standard* versions of the Bible) eat the crumbs of their masters that the Biblical Jesus agreed to heal her daughter.

The Biblical Jesus revealed also what can be perceived as ethnocentrism when he commanded his disciples not to preach to Gentiles or Samaritans but to go instead "to the people of Israel—God's lost sheep" (Matthew 10:5–6). A similar attitude of partiality appears to be revealed in John 4:22, where Jesus is represented as saying that "we Jews know all about him [God], for salvation comes to the world through the Jews." Further, the Biblical Jesus taught in parables so that people "outside the kingdom" would "not understand or turn to God, or be forgiven for their sins." Thus, his disciples "are permitted to know some truths about the kingdom of God that are hidden to those outside the kingdom" (Mark 4:11–12). Those latter verses have been treated as fulfilling Isaiah 6:9–10, in which God commands Isaiah to tell his people that "Though you watch and watch as I perform my miracles, still you don't know what they mean." The Biblical God then instructs Isaiah to "Dull their understanding, close their eyes and shut their eyes. . . . I don't want them to see or to hear or to understand, or to turn to me to heal them."

Jesus is also depicted as displaying discourtesy. Consider the following story, in which at least questionable means are used to achieve the worthy goal of warning people against hypocrisy:

> As he was speaking, one of the Pharisees asked him home for a meal. When Jesus arrived, he sat down to eat without first performing the

> ceremonial washing required by Jewish custom. That greatly sur-
> prised his host. Then Jesus said to him, "You Pharisees wash the out-
> side, but inside you are still dirty—full of greed and wickedness!
> Fools! Didn't God make the inside as well as the outside? Purity is best
> demonstrated by generosity. Woe to you Pharisees! (Luke 11:37–40)

Jesus is described as verbally abusing his host for hypocrisy,
while he himself gives expression to disrespect, discourtesy,
and vituperation. Further, the Biblical Jesus might be seen as
discourteous and disrespectful to Peter, when the latter inter-
vened to protect him. To Peter the Biblical Jesus said, "Get
away from me, you Satan! You are a dangerous trap to me."
(Matthew 16:23) Although Jesus, according to the Bible, was
determined to be sacrificed, it seems as though he could have
displayed more understanding and appreciation for Peter's
concern. That remark is particularly surprising when it is considered that the Biblical Jesus had previously promised to give
Peter "the keys to the Kingdom of Heaven", declaring that
Peter was "a stone; and upon this rock I will build my church"
(Matthew 16:18–19).

It is perhaps ironic that many Christian fundamentalists
view Jesus as having favored close and strong families, when
most of the remarks ascribed to him in the Bible appear to
show him as at the least unconcerned about that institution.
Indeed, there are some Biblical references that give plausible
reason for thinking that Jesus was sometimes even hostile to
the family unit, and saw it as almost inimical to the following
of his teachings. Although the Biblical Jesus' teachings on divorce were strict, he often made remarks that might easily be
seen as showing his indifference to family ties. In Luke 14:26
Jesus is quoted as saying:

> Anyone who wants to be my follower must love me far more than he
> does his own father, mother, wife, children, brothers, or sisters—yes,
> more than his own life—otherwise he cannot be my disciple. [Note
> that in the King James and Revised Standard versions of the Bible Jesus
> commands his disciples to "hate" their families.]

The Biblical Jesus sometimes did not appear concerned that
his words might either help to destroy families or cause people not to be concerned about the stability of their families:

> I have come to set a man against his father, and a daughter against her
> mother, and a daughter-in-law against her mother-in-law—a man's

worst enemies will be right in his own home! If you love your father and mother more than you love me, you are not worthy of being mine; or if you love your son or daughter more than me, you are not worthy of being mine. (Matthew 10:35–37)

Note also that the Bible reports the following incident in which the Biblical Jesus evidently ignored his family, virtually disowning them:

As Jesus was speaking in a crowded house his mother and brothers were outside, wanting to talk with him. When someone told him they were there, he remarked, "Who is my mother? Who are my brothers?" He pointed to his disciples. "Look!" he said, "these are my mother and brothers." Then he added, "Anyone who obeys my Father in heaven is my brother, sister and mother!" (Matthew 12:46–50)

While most of the Bible tends to represent fidelity to one's parents as important and certainly quite compatible with serving God, the Biblical Jesus often spoke as if serving God and honoring one's parents were naturally antagonistic. It does not seem that he simply wanted to stress the importance of serving God over all other ends. For the predominant tone reflected in the Biblical Jesus' remarks on the family can easily lead one to believe that he thought that gaining salvation and honoring one's parents were often incompatible. Consider the following:

Brother shall betray brother to death, and fathers shall betray their own children. And children shall rise against their parents and cause their deaths. (Matthew 10:21)

Of course, the statement may have been a realistic prediction of what often occurred when family members differed in their choices of paths to spiritual enlightenment. Yet when taken along with the Biblical Jesus' other statements about the family, it can suggest that he was not much concerned about family unity. Indeed, he sometimes, in effect, offered rewards to people who acted in such a way as to break up their families:

And anyone who gives up his home, brothers, sisters, father, mother, wife, children, or property, to follow me, shall receive a hundred times as much in return, and shall have eternal life. (Matthew 19:29)

Notwithstanding the message of many Christian fundamentalists, the words just quoted do not appear to be the words of someone concerned with preserving and strengthening the institution of the family.

In Matthew 10:34, the Biblical Jesus said: "Don't imagine that I came to bring peace to the earth! No, rather, a sword." Unfortunately, some of the actions ascribed to the Biblical Jesus seem to support the statement. For it is possible to interpret him as having at least twice participated in wanton destruction. On one occasion the Biblical Jesus destroyed a herd of pigs as a consequence of an exorcism:

> A herd of pigs was feeding in the distance, so the demons begged, "If you cast us out, send us into that herd of pigs." "All right," Jesus told them. "Begone." And they came out of the men and entered the pigs, and the whole herd rushed over the cliff and drowned in the water below. (Matthew 8:28–32; Mark 5:1–3; Luke 8:26–33)

Instead of harmlessly banishing the demons, the Biblical Jesus let them destroy someone's inoffensive animals.

On another occasion, the Biblical Jesus appeared to reveal a wanton destructiveness when he cursed and destroyed a fig tree because it did not bear fruit *out of season:*

> In the morning, as he was returning to Jerusalem, he was hungry, and noticed a fig tree beside the road. He went over to see if there were many figs, but there were only leaves [for it was too early in the season (Mark 11:13)]. Then he said to it, "Never bear fruit again!" And soon the fig tree withered up. (Matthew 21:18–19)

He then assured his disciples that through faith they too could have similar powers of destruction, ". . . and much more. You can even say to this mountain of olives 'Move over into the ocean' and it will." (Matthew 21:21) While Matthew might be seen as interpreting the story of the fig tree to emphasize the power of faith, his interpretation makes Jesus appear to have wrought needless destruction. As described by Matthew, the story might be regarded as less than flattering to Jesus, who is represented as using dubious methods to illustrate the power of faith.

While Matthew probably interpreted the story of the fig tree largely if not principally to show the power of faith, Mark appears to have interpreted it more negatively, to demonstrate the price of religious disobedience or disbelief. Perhaps the most common interpretation of Mark's use of the story views the fig tree as representing the Temple of Jerusalem, destroyed for its disbelief in Jesus. Biblical scholars Norman Perrin and Dennis C. Duling write:

> Mark 11:11–25 is an interesting example of the author's compositional technique, because he interprets the cleansing of the Temple (11:15–19) by intercalating it into the account of the cursing of the fig tree (11:12–14, 20–25). Mark thus comes to terms with the catastrophe of the destruction of the Temple [in A.D. 70] by understanding it as the judgment of God on a place become unworthy and by seeing the tradition of Jesus' cleansing the Temple as anticipating that judgment. [*The New Testament: An Introduction* (New York: Harcourt, Brace, Jovanovich, 1982), p.251]

Accepting the Biblical Jesus' curse as an unqualified condemnation of anyone who does not accept his Messiahship may be seen as denouncing people for their beliefs, even if they have based their beliefs on an honest attempt to appraise the relevant evidence. So interpreted, Mark's account of the fig tree curse has significant anti-intellectual implications. For cursing people for their beliefs, regardless of how they arrived at them, conflicts with the ideal of rationality, which requires a commitment to reason and the free and sustained use of the mind. That ideal generally requires people dispassionately to investigate all relevant claims and evidence in search of the truth and to avoid sacrificing honest conclusions to the demands or threats of other people. From the standpoint of rationality, one's thinking is reprehensible only if it is deliberately slipshod, only if it does not reflect a sincere attempt critically to discover the truth. That ideal is well expressed by Thomas Jefferson, who said that people will be judged not by the rightness but by the uprightness of their beliefs.

Unfortunately, on a plausible reading of Mark, the Biblical Jesus' curse can easily be interpreted as categorically condemning people solely because they do not believe in him, regardless of their honest appraisal of the evidence for his Messianic claims. That interpretation also harmonizes with some other parts of the New Testament, particularly the Pauline epistles, in which "natural man's" reliance on reason in matters of religious belief is categorically denounced (for example, 1 Corinthians 1:18–29; 2:14; 3:18–21).

JESUS' TEACHING METHOD

That interpretation of the curse also harmonizes well with the way in which the Gospels sometimes depict Jesus' conception of himself. The Biblical Jesus' method of teaching, or convincing, people was "as one who had great authority" (Matthew 7:29). He impressed people by the self-confidence with which he presented his views, which were represented as coming directly from God. The Biblical Jesus, in other words, presented himself as having privileged access to God's mind. Although Jesus came from a tradition in which people commonly represented themselves as Divine spokespersons, that tradition often encouraged uncritical acceptance of other people's views and discouraged the free use of the mind.

As the following quotations indicate, the teaching style of the Biblical Jesus at times called for categorical, unquestioning acceptance with no toleration for disagreement:

Anyone who wants to be my follower must love me. . . . (Luke 14:26)

With all the earnestness I have I say: . . . if anyone breaks the least commandment, and teaches others to, he shall be the least in the kingdom of heaven. (Matthew 5:18–19)

But if anyone publicly denies me I will openly deny him before my Father in heaven. (Matthew 10:33)

Anyone who isn't helping me is harming me. (Matthew 12:30)

And of course you should obey their [the Jewish leaders' and Pharisees'] every whim! (Matthew 23:3)

I am the light of the world. So if you follow me, you won't be stumbling in the darkness, . . . (John 8:12)

Further, according to John's interpretation of the Biblical Jesus' message, "all who trust him—God's Son—to save them have eternal life; those who don't believe and obey shall never see heaven, but the wrath of God remains upon them" (John 3:36). The Biblical Jesus, therefore, is "Master" and "Lord" (John 13:13), "Teacher" (John 13:14), and parent-substitute (Luke 14:26).

Unfortunately, the Biblical Jesus' presenting himself as an unquestionable authority can have the effect of depreciating individual judgment. That depreciation of individual judgment was one of the most important respects in which the teaching style of the Biblical Jesus differed from, for example, that of the Buddha. The Buddha, who lived over five hundred years before Jesus, rebelled against many Hindu beliefs and values, including Hindu authoritarianism. When Hindus were uncritically relying on the Brahmins to tell them how to live, the Buddha challenged each person to do his own seeking and thinking:

> Do not accept what you hear by report, do not accept tradition, do not accept a statement because it is found in our books, nor because it is in accord with your belief, nor because it is the saying of your teacher. . . . Be ye lamps unto yourselves. . . . Those who, either now or after I am dead, shall rely upon themselves only and not look for assistance to anyone besides themselves, it is they who shall reach the very topmost height. [E.A. Burtt, ed., *The Teachings of the Compassionate Buddha* (New York: Mentor Books, 1955), pp.49–50]

> When you know of yourselves: "These teachings are not good: these teachings when followed out and put in practice conduce to loss and suffering"—then reject them. [Quoted in F.L. Woodward, *Some Sayings of the Buddha* (London: Oxford University Press, 1939), p.283]

Unlike the Biblical Jesus, the Buddha went out of his way to emphasize the value of individual judgment. The point here is not to address the merits or deficiencies of Buddhism. Indeed, a comprehensive understanding of the Buddha would require a careful study of the intellectual climate of Hindu India. The point, however, is to emphasize that the Biblical Jesus at times commanded uncritical obedience to authority using a teaching style that contrasted sharply with one like that of the Buddha, who taught a respect for individual intelligence and experience. Accordingly, the Biblical Jesus at times required people to believe in and follow him, apparently regardless of their individual judgment of his teaching.

Whether all the Biblical Jesus' *teachings* were perfect is not the issue here; it is, rather, that the Bible seems to imply that he adopted an imperfect *method* of teaching. To make clearer the problem with part of his method of teaching, consider two styles of teaching about, for example, the causes of the Civil War.

The most effective teacher who tries to explain the causes of the Civil War will point out the enormous complexity of its causes and explain the many different ways of viewing them. He will encourage his students to ask questions and to support their views with reasons. If the teacher maintains, for example, that President Lincoln was concerned more with preserving the Union than with abolishing slavery, he will cite reasons for his belief and will not unconditionally condemn the students for disagreeing with him.

The least effective teacher will maintain that only *his* answers can possibly be right, and that it is immoral for his students to question him. He will condemn any intellectual independence as subversive, and if the students insist that there are different ways to view the problem from the ways the teacher suggests, he will threaten them with torment for their 'nonconformity'. That teacher will see his students as unalterably incompetent to think for themselves, and will in short do everything he can to create carbon copies of himself. The teacher is the master, and his students are only his slaves. The result will probably be that they will accept any proposition the teacher advances, and hope that it is true. Even if it is true, they might not understand why it is true, and their knowledge of other aspects of the proposition will be severely limited. Lastly, they will be in petrified fear of their teacher, and their desire to use their minds for any other endeavor might be stifled.

Like that teacher, the Biblical Jesus can be interpreted as not having inspired his supposedly unintelligent students (disciples) with self-confidence; in fact, he seemed at times to discourage exploring other avenues—right and wrong—to the answer. He also apparently threatened them with extreme suffering if they doubted what he said.

SOME CONTROVERSIAL TEACHINGS OF JESUS

Jesus, as presented in the Bible, almost certainly accepted and taught a belief in endless punishment. Indeed, many fundamentalists as well as non-fundamentalists do believe in eternal punishment. Some people, however, attempt to defend the idea of only limited punishment by citing certain Biblical verses.

These defenders sometimes point to Luke 12:47–48, where Jesus is presented as saying that servants who understand their Master but do not serve him well will receive a severe beating, whereas servants who do not know they are not following their Master's wishes will receive a light beating. On the basis of that verse, it has been suggested that the Biblical Jesus taught that punishment will be proportioned to the degree of guilt.

To argue for the possibility of limited punishment, it is possible to cite also Matthew 5:25–26, where Jesus is presented as saying that, unless one reaches a settlement with his creditors before the final stage of trial, he will not leave prison until he has paid the last penny. This verse may suggest that Jesus taught that once people have paid their debts for their sins, their punishment will cease.

Further, it is conceivable that, since the Biblical Jesus taught that there is only one unpardonable sin (Matthew 12:32), other sins may be forgiven.

Finally, some people note that the New Testament word 'aionios', usually translated 'everlasting' or 'eternal', can also mean 'for the aeon, or age'.

Yet while those interpretations of verses in the Bible are most likely a comfort to people who do not believe in eternal punishment, and while all people should seek what is most meaningful to them in the Bible, such interpretations do not establish that the Biblical Jesus taught belief in only limited punishment.

Indeed, the Biblical Jesus never explicitly taught that punishment was less than everlasting, and the overwhelming likelihood is that he taught and believed in eternal punishment. For although it is true that the New Testament word 'aionios' can mean 'for the aeon, or age', it is doubtful to interpret it thus in comments about Hell, just as it is doubtful to interpret comments about Heaven as implying that union with God will be only 'for the aeon, or age'.

Further, the Biblical Jesus is hardly ever described as showing much compassion for those people he believed deserved Hell, which he described in horrific terms: "eternal fire" (Matthew 25:41), "never-ending fire" (Matthew 3:12), and "furnace" (Matthew 13:42), in which there is "weeping and gnashing of teeth" (Matthew 8:12; 13:42, 50; 22:13; 24:51; 25:30; Luke 13:28). The Biblical Jesus seems to have accepted without question the language of his contemporaries, apparently using the language of Hell to warn people against those qualities of character eternally condemned by God (for example, Matthew 25:41–46).

With all these points honestly considered, it can be acknowledged that even if Jesus himself did not believe in, and teach belief in, an everlasting Hell, the strong language on that topic attributed to him in the Bible has historically had the effect of frightening, and in some cases brutalizing, a large number of people throughout Christendom. In short, throughout history most people have interpreted the Biblical Jesus as having taught a belief in endless punishment.

Moral Questions for Fundamentalists

The question arises: Is eternal punishment really the plan of the all-merciful God, or was the Biblical Jesus simply mistaken? It is difficult to see the point and the morality of endlessly torturing people. Pain is presumptively bad, and it is desirable only when the infliction of it is necessary for a greater good, such as reforming criminals or deterring potential criminals from crime. Endless torture, however, is not designed to reform people, nor is the threat of it necessarily effective at deterring people from harming others. Torture, war, corruption, and murder were rampant, for example, throughout the Middle Ages, when people were filled with the belief in, and fear of, Hell. Indeed, the *belief* in Hell has, in itself, often yielded persecution, torture, and murder.

By thinking that they must believe in Hell to affirm their faith in God, many fundamentalists are liable to view God as limited in power or in goodness. They may force themselves to ask questions that impugn God's love and perfection: 'Is the power of God limited?' 'Is His power to save people limited?' 'Why then does He place people in Hell rather than saving them?' 'Is God's goodness limited?' 'If He does not want to save them, then why must He make them suffer eternally in the evil of Hell, making no effort to redeem such evil?'

Many non-fundamentalists choose not to accept the Biblical Jesus' view of Hell because they believe that it would show that either God's goodness or His power has limits. They reason that if God could not ultimately save everyone, He would not be all-powerful, and if He did not want to save everyone, He would not be all-good, since He would be allowing the evil of endless torture to continue, unredeemed by any compensatory good. Morally speaking, almost any other treatment of the wicked is preferable to endless torture, in which finite crimes receive infinite punishment. Even the annihilation of the unsaved would be less morally objectionable than an endless Hell. Yet, indeed, expecting anything less than universal salvation may conceivably be an insulting portrayal of God. For it is unlikely that a morally perfect God could feel the all-too-human desire for revenge in His master plan.

Yet it appears that not only did the Biblical Jesus portray God as sending some people to eternal, unredeemed suffering, but also he suggested that there is at least one sin that can never be forgiven: "Even blasphemy against me or any other sin, can be forgiven—all except one: speaking against the Holy Spirit shall never be forgiven, either in this world or in the world to come" (Matthew 12:32). That is the 'unpardonable sin' expressed in a verse that has caused great fear and anguish to many of its devout readers because they either did not know whether they had committed the sin or did not believe they had any hope of being spared from eternal Hell.

WHO GOES TO HELL AND WHO IS SPARED?

Suppose some people have devoted all their lives to helping others and being kind to all whom they knew. Presumably, God, who is infinite in justness and righteousness, would reward them with salvation. Yet some passages present Jesus as at least implying that such people would be damned, caused to suffer forever in Hell, if they did not accept Jesus as their Saviour.

Consider the following statements that John attributes to Jesus:

There is no eternal doom awaiting those who trust him to save them. But those who don't trust him have already been tried and condemned for not believing in the only Son of God. (John 3:18)

And the Father leaves all judgement of sin to his Son, so that everyone will honor the Son, just as they honor the Father. But if you refuse to honor God's Son, whom he sent to you, then you are certainly not honoring the Father. (5:22–23)

No one can get to the Father except by means of me [Jesus]. (14:6)

This spirit of religious intolerance, as well as the severe limiting of the availability of salvation, is also sometimes shown in the words attributed to Jesus in the Gospels of Matthew, Mark, and Luke. As pointed out earlier, the Biblical Jesus referred to non-Jews as "dogs" (Matthew 15:26) and at least one time forbade his followers to preach to Gentiles. In Luke 13:24–25, the Biblical Jesus said, "The door to heaven is narrow. Work hard to get in, for the truth is that many will try to enter but when the head of the house has locked the door, it will be too late. Then if you stand outside knocking, and pleading, 'Lord, open the door for us,' he will reply, 'I do not know you. . . . You can't come in here, guilty as you are. Go away.' And there will be great weeping and gnashing of teeth as you stand outside. . . ." In Matthew 10:33, the Biblical Jesus said: "If anyone publicly denies me, I will openly deny him before my Father in heaven." Further, in Mark 16:16, Jesus is represented as saying, "Those who believe and are baptized will be saved. But those who refuse to believe will be condemned." The ideas expressed in those verses have, when accepted as literally inerrant, tended to inspire intolerance and division among people; none of them stresses love and justice over ritual and dogma. When asked "What should we do to satisfy God?", the Biblical Jesus' only reply, according to John, was, "This is the work of God, that you believe in him whom he has sent" (6:28–29).

With a narrow understanding of a number of intolerant-sounding verses, most fundamentalists risk viewing as perfect a plan of salvation in which both Adolf Hitler (a murderer of millions) and Thomas Jefferson (who rejected Christianity) are to be punished equally, a plan in which love and justice alone cannot save anyone from endless torture.

Salvation might require, for example, belief in Jesus' sacrificial atonement (Matthew 10:33; Mark 16:16; John 3:16–18). Or, for example, as the Biblical Jesus said in John 6:53–54: "Unless you eat the flesh of the Messiah and drink his blood, you cannot have eternal life within you. But anyone who does eat my flesh and drink my blood has eternal life."

Of course, most non-fundamentalists can feel free to believe that the Bible may not inerrantly represent Jesus' teachings. Thus, non-fundamentalists can, if they so choose, believe that in reality Jesus did *not* believe in, or teach belief in, eternal damnation. Certainly, it is possible that he did rise above the most morally questionable belief of his culture. For although it was the prevailing Jewish belief of his day and the language of Hell was common, belief in Hell did not *have* to be accepted by Jesus. Indeed, it was not accepted by all Jews of that time. The Sadducees, for example, did not believe in immortality, and a number of Jewish teachers explicitly taught a doctrine of limited punishment. Thus, Rabbi Akiba (A.D. 50–132) taught: "The punishment of the wicked in Gehinnom lasts twelve months; for it is written [Isaiah 66:23]: It will be from month to [the same] month." That non-literal interpretation was accepted in the Mishnah (Eduyyoth 2:10) and assumed elsewhere in the Talmud (for example, Sabbath 33b and 152b).

It is not unreasonable or irreverent to acknowledge that there would be very little, if any, moral justification for endless torture, particularly the endless torture of millions, if not billions, of people whose damned or damning crime was supposedly the failure to acknowledge that the Son of God had already saved them. Clearly, such penalty would be opposed to any sense of justice that most human beings possess, and would certainly be opposed to the sense of justice that has been endorsed in numerous verses in the Bible. For example, according to Micah, God demands "only to do justice, to love mercy, and to walk humbly with your God" (Micah 6:8). And Isaiah represented God as disgusted with animal sacrifices, demanding justice instead:

> Bring no more vain offerings; incense is an abomination to me . . . ; wash yourselves; make yourselves clean; remove the evil of your doings from before my eyes; cease to do evil, learn to do good, seek jus-

tice, abolish oppression; defend the orphan, plead for the widow. (Isaiah 1:11–17)

And in the Book of Jonah, for example, God decides not to destroy the once wicked city of Nineveh, because everyone there repents (turns "from his evil ways, from his violence and robbing") after being threatened with destruction (Jonah 3:8). Jonah expresses displeasure that God had spared the city, but his desire for punishment stands in stark contrast to God's attitude of compassion: "Why shouldn't I feel sorry for a great city like Nineveh with its 120,000 people in utter spiritual darkness, and its cattle?" (Jonah 4:11) Where Jonah saw enemies and sinners, God saw fragile people who stumbled but who tried to stand up again. Where Jonah desired revenge, God forgave the people of Nineveh simply because they repented of their wickedness, though they had not been converted, circumcised, or baptized. In short, He forgave these former enemies of the Israelites simply because they tried to be more decent and loving human beings. The spirit informing the story of Jonah is predominantly one of mercy and universalism; through the ages its message has been taken as illustrating that God loves and forgives people regardless of their religion or ethnic heritage. Thus, in some of the verses found in the story of Jonah and in Micah and Isaiah, as well as in other parts of the Bible, theology and ritual are downplayed, and justice and righteousness are especially emphasized.

CONCLUSION

Many fundamentalists, then, may ultimately risk sacrificing a more nearly balanced view of the Biblical Jesus for a wooden and narrow view of the Bible. Their adherence to the doctrine of Biblical inerrancy permits them to recognize that Jesus may have possessed many valuable attributes, such as the capacity for love and forgiveness, and that he has been an inspiration to millions, but that adherence may deny them the ability to perceive the dimension of the Bible that presents Jesus as sometimes expressing vindictiveness, discourtesy, narrowmindedness, and ethnic and religious intolerance.

The notion that the Bible presents Jesus as having perfect wisdom is not, however, the only controversial idea that many fundamentalists are liable to accept to maintain their doctrine of Biblical inerrancy. For, as will be seen in the next chapter, a number of misleading notions have developed among many fundamentalists, as well as non-fundamentalists, about key aspects of the Bible.

CHAPTER 8

POPULAR MISCONCEPTIONS ABOUT THE BIBLE

T he Bible is a complex and multi-faceted work, most enriching when it is approached without preconceived notions. Yet almost inevitably, a number of misconceptions about the Bible, including claims about inspiration and infallibility, accuracy and completeness, unity and uniqueness, and so on, have been formed. Although many religious people can reject those misleading notions without feeling that their Christian faith is threatened, the majority of fundamentalists are particularly susceptible to holding those notions, especially the notion that the Bible claims itself to be inerrant. If one labors under any false impressions about the Bible, the ability to feel confident that each verse is being understood and interpreted in the most appropriate and sensitive way may be ultimately at risk. Consider, then, the following discussion about some of the more popular Biblical misconceptions.

DOES THE BIBLE CLAIM TO BE INFALLIBLE?

Are there any verses in the Bible stating that every word of the Bible is directly inspired by God ("God-breathed"), and that the Bible is *totally* reliable and inerrant? While the Bible does contain many very beautiful, inspiring, and practical verses, nowhere does the Bible claim complete inerrancy, nor does it clearly claim total, direct inspiration. The four verses that come closest seemingly to claiming either inspiration or inerrancy fall short of any kind of proof:

(1) 2 Timothy 3:16: [Paul:] "The whole Bible was given to us by inspiration from God and is useful to teach us what is true. . . ."

That is perhaps the most-cited Biblical verse in support of the doctrines of inspiration and inerrancy. Yet there are few verses more debated than that.

One part of the debate relates to the phrase, "The whole Bible." Here, the Greek, "pasa graphē", literally 'every Scripture', makes the beginning of the sentence read (roughly) as either "Every Scripture is inspired by God and is useful . . ." or "Every inspired Scripture is useful. . . ." The latter reading, therefore, would refer to *only* whatever passages or books of Scripture are inspired. The former reading would indicate that *all* Scripture is inspired. Greek-language experts are divided over which is the most proper translation. Only one thing is certain: They will never know for certain what was the author's intention.

The word "Bible" in that phrase is another key part of the debate. Taken from the Greek, "graphē", it literally means 'writing' or 'book', but the context of previous verses generally implies that "graphē" refers only to the Old Testament. The previous verse relates to "hiera grammata" (sacred writings), which was a common designation for the Old Testament in that day. Some commentators maintain that those two phrases could also refer to Christian writings, but that assumption ignores the context of the verses, which nowhere directly refer to any Christian writings. It also does not consider that the concept of a 'New Testament' did not exist before at least late in the second century.

'Inspiration from God' is still another phrase that has fuelled the debate. The Greek, "theopneustos", translates roughly as 'breathed by God', and the phrase is not found in any other part of the Bible. Since there is no other Biblical use against which to compare it, its exact theological meaning cannot be established. Breath, of course, is the manner in which Man speaks; God is depicted as having breathed the breath of life into Man (Genesis 2); and God, therefore, has provided all humankind with the means to breathe, and thus to speak. In that sense, perhaps, the people of the Bible were 'inspired' by God. Whether "theopneustos" means any more, or less, than that is a subject of continuing debate.

Lastly, the mere statement that something inspired by God is *useful* to teach what is true is not equivalent to saying that everything in the Bible is categorically free from any error.

It is indeed remarkable that support for the doctrine of inspiration—and therefore, presumably, of inerrancy—of the Bible could rest on a verse that is both enormously vague and enormously confusing. For here is illustrated, as well as any of the most difficult verses in the Bible, the immense complexity and confusing nature of translating what fundamentalists require themselves to view as the inerrant communication of God. Even if this verse was, in fact, a statement attesting to Biblical inspiration and inerrancy, is it plausible that this is the way used by the all-knowing God to say simply that He is speaking to you and me?

(2) 2 Peter 1:19–21: "So we have seen and proved that what the prophets said came true. You will do well to pay close attention to everything they have written, for, . . . their words help us to understand many things. . . . For no prophecy recorded in Scripture was ever thought up by the prophet himself. It was the Holy Spirit within these godly men who gave them true messages from God."

That verse refers to the prophecies of the prophets, and says nothing about the historical data in the Old Testament or anything written in the New Testament.

It says to "pay close attention" to what the prophets wrote; it does not say that the writing itself was directed by God, much less that it was inerrant, or even that everything written in the name of the prophets was accurate.

(3) Matthew 5:17–18 (similarly in Luke 16:16–17): [Jesus said,] "Don't misunderstand why I have come—it isn't to cancel the laws of Moses and the warnings of the prophets. No, I came to fulfill them, and to make them all come true. . . . Every law in the Book will continue until its purpose is achieved. And so if anyone breaks the least commandment, and teaches others to, he shall be least in the Kingdom of Heaven. But those who teach God's laws *and obey them* shall be great in the Kingdom of Heaven."

Again, that makes no allusion to the 'New Testament' portion of the Bible.

It refers to the actual laws and prophecies of the Old Testament, not to general historical accounts.

And it makes no claim about the absolute inerrancy of everything written in the Bible.

(4) Mark 13:31: [Jesus said,] "Heaven and earth shall disappear, but my words stand sure forever."

The "words" here refer directly to the preceding sentence: "Yes, these are the events that will signal the end of the age."

Even if the "words" refer to all Jesus' words as recorded in the Bible, one must keep in mind that those words constitute a small percentage of what is written in the Bible.

No reference to *written* words is suggested, only that what Jesus is *telling* the people will hold true (indeed, at the time, no words of Jesus had yet been recorded). There is therefore no attestation that the written recording of these words and all the other words of the Bible have been superintended by God.

Indeed, it would have been inappropriate for Jesus to have stated that he believed every word of the Old and New Testaments to be absolutely true. For Jesus himself specifically advised against the law of Moses that said "an eye for an eye . . ." recommending in its stead, to "turn the other cheek . . ." (Matthew 5:38). Further, on the basis of John 8, one can reasonably conclude that the Biblical Jesus opposed the Levitical (20:10) death penalty for adulterers. Certainly, Jesus, as well as various New Testament authors, challenged (even if they did not discard) a number of Biblical laws (see Chapter 9).

Those four verses (mentioned above) are the most frequently used claims for either inspiration or Biblical inerrancy. If those do not establish inerrancy or at least inspiration, then the remaining verses are even less applicable. These verses represent the kinds of verses often used to try to support inerrancy: Exodus 4:14–16; Numbers 12:6–8; 16:28–30; 24:13; Deuteronomy 4:2; 18:1, 15; 2 Samuel 23:2; Psalms 19:7; 119:160; Proverbs 3:5–6; Isaiah 8:20; 51:9; Matthew 4:7, 10; 10:19–20; 22:29–32; Luke 12:11–12; 16:16–17; 24:27, 44, 45; John 5:46–47; 22:16–17; Acts 3:21; 1:16; 10:34–36; 19:24;

20:31; 24:14; 1 Corinthians 10:1, 11; 14:37; 1 Thessalonians 2:13; Hebrews 1:1; 10:15–16; James 4:5; 1 Peter 1:23–25; 2 Peter 3:15–16; Revelation 22:18–19.

When you read over those and other verses, you should keep the following considerations in mind:

1. No verse indicates that the particular *writers* of the Bible were inspired by God, much less caused to be inerrant in their writings.

2. While there are verses attesting to God's giving prophets and law-givers the words to say, there are no verses that attest to God's giving the *recorders* of such events/ prophecies/statements infallible inspiration. There is no claim that the written record of these sayings is perfectly accurate.

3. While there are verses acknowledging the method by which the messages of the Bible were originally inspired, there are no verses acknowledging that all the writers of all those messages were likewise inspired.

4. While there are also verses discussing the "Word" of God or "my word", those usually refer only to the immediate reference and deal with the message(s) *spoken* from God or Jesus, not to any *written* word.

5. While there are verses in which Jesus himself refers to Old Testament passages in the form 'it is written . . .' or 'the Scriptures tell . . .', those affirm at most only that the particular Old Testament verses being referred to are true or at least that they exist and are presumably useful; such verses say nothing about the inerrancy of either those passages or any other Old Testament passages.

6. While there are also verses affirming that certain prophecies have been, or will be, fulfilled, those verses say nothing of the absolute inerrancy of the *written* version of either those "prophecies" or any other "prophecies" in the Bible.

7. While there are also verses referring to the 'truth' or 'purity' of certain prophecies or messages, again there is no reference to the inerrancy of the recorder of such prophecies or messages.

8. While there are verses in which an apostle or prophet says that he believes in the Jewish law and everything written in the books of prophecy, those only attest to that individual's

belief, say nothing of New Testament laws and prophecies, and make no claims that all the Bible was inspired by God.

9. While there are also verses indicating that the "Word(s) of God" came from the prophets and law-givers, there is not one saying that those "Words" were accurately recorded in the Bible.

10. While there are verses proclaiming that the prophets and law-givers were inspired by God, there is not one saying that the *writers* were so inspired.

11. While there are some verses proclaiming that the 'prophecy' or message of the particular book of the Bible should not be changed or should not be ignored, no verse attests to the infallibility of all the words in that book, much less in the entire Bible.

12. While there are verses advising that "the law and the prophets" should not be altered, and that the law will not be changed until it is fulfilled, the phrase 'the Law' refers only to the laws found in the five books of Moses, the phrase 'the Prophets' refers only to the prophecies made by the prophets, and neither phrase refers to any of the Old Testament's historical or poetical books.

13. While there are some verses referring to the Scriptures as not having been written 'in vain' or not being capable of being 'broken', such designations, though referring to the overall usefulness and significance of the Old Testament, make no allusion to Old Testament infallibility.

14. While there is even a verse (Jeremiah 36:1–6) in which God directs a prophet to "Get a scroll and write down all my messages" from the days of Josiah up to Jeremiah's day, the subsequent verses indicate that even in this instance "Jeremiah dictated" to Baruch, and "Baruch wrote down all the prophecies", so that there is no indication that Baruch, the writer, was himself inspired by God and thus inerrant in his recording.

15. Lastly, it should be noted that nowhere in the historical portions of the Old Testament does the writer clearly make any claims of being God's scribe; it is only the prophets that ever identify their spoken statements as God's utterances.

While most fundamentalists believe that the Bible says that all the Bible is directly inspired by God, nowhere is any such categorical statement clearly evident. What is more, the claim of Biblical inerrancy is even further removed from the text of the Bible. Indeed, few if any Biblical scholars, including fundamentalist scholars, hold that the Bible explicitly testifies to its inerrancy. For most scholars realize that the notion of inerrancy is essentially a philosophical conclusion or inference, based on the assumption that if God inspires something, it must be free from error.

In any case, even if there were Biblical statements claiming inspiration or inerrancy, they could not be their own proof. There must be some outside evidence—that is, something other than the Bible itself—to establish the likelihood that the statements are true. In other words, it would make very little sense to believe that every sentence in a particular book was inerrant simply because a sentence or sentences in that book said that every sentence was inerrant. Such reasoning would be circular.

Fundamentalists, then, risk falling into that circle. Yet many non-fundamentalists who reject the doctrine of Biblical inerrancy are still often able to retain a strong Christian faith. Many people who, for example, consider themselves 'liberal Christians' are often very deeply devoted to God even though they do not view the Bible as inerrant. The intent here is not to advocate one particular religious belief over another, but rather to suggest one possible option for fundamentalists who are considering rejecting belief in the inerrancy of the Bible but who wish to retain a very strong Christian faith.

Many liberal Christians believe that believing the *exact* words ascribed to Jesus and God is less important than living in accordance with the central ethical messages embodied in some of those words. For many of these people written words can inspire, but they become real and true only when they are treated as a means to attaining the end of Godly morality and love.

Fundamentalists, however, who adopt a doctrine of Biblical inerrancy, risk being unable to adapt their religious beliefs *in any way* to the difficulties presented by such a doctrine. Thus, they also may be liable not fully to recognize what most other religious people can accept while retaining genuine reverence, even unflinching faith: that the exact words of Jesus and God need not be guaranteed to be contained in the Bible. People who do not require that the Bible be inerrant can easily recognize, for example, that there is no evidence that Jesus himself wrote any of the Bible, nor is there any evidence that he commanded anyone to write the books constituting the New Testament. The earliest Gospel (probably Mark) was written a few decades after Jesus died, in a language (Greek) in which he probably never preached. And although Paul's letters were written before the Gospel of Mark, Paul met Jesus only in a vision.

WHO WROTE THE BIBLE?

Are the actual authors of the Bible the people who the Bible claims to be the authors? Note that *The Book* (the version of the Bible from which verses are quoted herein) acknowledges that, at least sometimes, the people who the Bible claims are the authors of particular writings are not the actual authors. In its introductory remarks on individual books of the Bible, *The Book* notes that the authors of the books of Esther (p.531), Job (p.540), and 1 and 2 Samuel (pp.288, 324) are unknown; that not all the Proverbs were written by Solomon (p.641); and that many of the Psalms were not written by David (p.568). *The Book* also admits to not being certain that Solomon wrote Ecclesiastes (p.668), or that Joshua wrote the book of Joshua (p.228). Many Biblical scholars believe that Moses was not the author of all the 'Five Books of Moses' (Genesis, Exodus, Leviticus, Numbers, Deuteronomy); that the books of Joshua, 1 and 2 Samuel, Song of Solomon, Daniel, Esther, Job, and Jonah were not written by the persons whose names are in the titles; that Lamentations was not written by Jeremiah; that Ecclesiastes was not written by Solomon; and that not all the Proverbs were by Solomon, nor all the book of Isaiah by Isaiah. In other words, despite Biblical traditions suggesting otherwise, many Biblical verses were not written by the people with whose names they have come to be associated.

The evidence leading to those conclusions is often not hard to find. Indeed, one need not be a Biblical scholar to discover partial evidence in the very pages of the Bible that at least some of those books were not written by the traditionally assigned authors. The following examples suggest that in order for some of those authors really to have been the authors, they must have either written the accounts many years after they had died, or simply made some peculiar, indeed bizarre, errors. (For additional evidence, please consult the suggested readings at the end of this book.)

1. Genesis 14:14 mentions the city of Dan. Yet in the days of Genesis, when Moses (the author?) lived, Dan was still called 'Laish'. As clearly indicated in Judges 18:27–29, the city did not become known as 'Dan' until the time of Judges (when the tribe of Dan conquered the city of Laish and changed its name).

2. Genesis 21:34 says that Abraham spent time in the "land of the Philistines", yet the Philistines did not enter Canaan until about 1150 B.C., about 500 years after Abraham's period (and thus considerably after the lifetime of Moses, the person traditionally credited with writing Genesis).

3. Genesis 36:31 refers to a period "before Israel had her first king", which was not until at least Saul's time, long after the supposed period of Moses and Genesis.

4. In Numbers 12:3, Moses is referred to as "the humblest man on earth", a strangely self-contradictory description for Moses (the author?) to have given himself.

5. In Deuteronomy 34:10, "There has never been another prophet like Moses", would be a strange remark for Moses to make, especially after he had already died.

6. In Deuteronomy 34:5–6, the author (Moses?) reports the events of Moses's having "died" and been "buried" by God. Further, 34:8 then states that "The people of Israel mourned for him for thirty days on the plains of Moab." Would a dead 'author' have been able to report such an event?

7. Joshua 7:1–8:29 refers to the Israelite conquest of the city of Ai, which, according to archaeological research, was not even an occupied city in the days of Joshua, the supposed author.

8. In 1 Samuel 25:1 and 28:3, references are made to the death and burial of Samuel (the author?), and the story continues through to the death of Saul (1 Samuel 31), who outlived Samuel, and through the subsequent, entire reign of King David (in 2 Samuel).

9. The 137th Psalm (of the 'Psalms of David') refers to Jewish captivity in Babylon. It is therefore clearly not of David's era, which was more than 400 years before any such Babylonian captivity.

IS THE BIBLE PERFECTLY ACCURATE?

Evidently the belief in perfect Biblical accuracy is also a misconception. For Leviticus 11:6 states that "the hare . . . chews the cud . . .", which is a demonstrably false biological statement.

Some New Testament writers refer to Old Testament verses and accounts that do not correlate with those references. For example, in Matthew 27:9, the author describes Jeremiah as the speaker of a particular quotation that in fact comes from the prophecy of Zechariah (in Zechariah 11:13), not Jeremiah. Still further, the author of Matthew's Gospel misreads Chronicles when, in Matthew 23:35, he refers to "Zechariah (son of Barachiah), slain by you in the Temple between the altar and the sanctuary." 2 Chronicles 24:20–22 explicitly states that Zechariah, who was executed in the court of the Temple, was the son of *Jehoiada*, not Barachiah.

DOES THE BIBLE PRESENT A SINGLE VIEWPOINT?

Is the Bible a perfect unit of thought? Any person who reads the whole Bible, without being told in advance that it is a work that is supposed to be *entirely* true, *entirely* in agreement, and *nowhere* contradictory, would have to conclude that it is a collection of strands of thought that sometimes conflict. The books of the Bible were written over more than a thousand years, and reflect the views of various cultures and numerous writers. For example, the beliefs, hopes, and attitudes embodied in the Old Testament book of Ecclesiastes diverge considerably from those often found in the New Testament. In Ecclesiastes one may plausibly infer that there is nothing to which people can look forward after death:

> It seems so unfair, that one fate comes to all. . . . there is nothing but death ahead anyway. There is hope only for the living. "It is better to be a live dog than a dead lion." For the living at least know that they will die! But the dead know nothing; they don't even have their memories. (Ecclesiastes 9:3–5)

Contrast those verses with a passage from First Corinthians:

> For our earthly bodies, the ones we have now that can die, must be transformed into heavenly bodies that cannot perish but will live forever.
>
> When this happens, then at last this Scripture will come true— "Death is swallowed up in victory." O death, where then your victory? Where then your sting? (1 Corinthians 15:53–55)

While the ideas of the resurrection of the dead and immortality have come to be enormously important in Christianity, the Bible shows a clear historical development of those ideas, which evolved over time; those ideas were not unchanging over the centuries.

The New Testament belief in the resurrection of the dead is only very rarely expressed in the Old Testament, where the dead are most often thought of not as being immortal but as leading a shadowy, insubstantial existence in Sheol, the netherworld. In fact, there are only two unambiguous references to resurrection in the Old Testament, Isaiah 26:19 and Daniel 12:2. So few and so late are those references in Scripture that the Sadducees of Jesus' day, who were strict observers of Scripture, did not even accept the idea of resurrection.

Throughout the Old Testament, the dead are pictured as shadows of their former selves and as living inside the earth in Sheol. Like the shades in Homer's *Iliad*, the 'rephaim' (ghosts or shadows) in the Old Testament were conceived on the model of vaporous bodies. Just as the shade of Patroklos in the *Iliad* was described as like his living self, so Samuel was described as having ascended from Sheol in visible presence (1 Samuel 28:3–25). In Sheol, Samuel was pictured as wearing his ghostly mantle, and kings were pictured as sitting on shadowy thrones (1 Samuel 28:14). Often regarded as the final abode of *everyone* (for example, Job 30:23), Sheol was dreary, a land of silence (Psalm 94:17), forgetfulness (Psalm 88:12), and destruction (Job 26:6), its inhabitants often conceived as neither knowing nor caring about matters on earth (Job 14:21–22). So far from being glorified, the inhabitants of Sheol, however great on earth, were at times described as weak in Sheol (Isaiah 14:9–10). Life in Sheol was at times considered so insubstantial as to approach non-existence (Psalm 39:13).

Sheol was often conceived not as a place of punishment but as a place of rest, where the wicked ceased from troubling and where the great as well as the small were free from earthly toils (Job 3:17–19). Throughout most of the Old Testament such hopes as the Hebrews had were quite this-worldly, concerning the Hebrew nation or one's offspring (Job 5:25). For Yahweh was presented as a God only of the living who did not exercise influence among the dead, who were without help (Psalm 88:3–5). Accordingly, Hezekiah believed that his death would separate him from Yahweh (Isaiah 38:18). Similarly convinced was the psalmist who said: "The dead praise not the Lord, neither any that go down into silence" (Psalm 115:17; *King James Version*).

Gradually some of the Hebrews came to believe that Yahweh would influence those in Sheol. Said Amos: "Though they dig into hell, thence shall my hand take them" (Amos 9:2; *King James Version*). Eventually Yahweh's power was viewed as extending to Sheol. Thus Isaiah could challenge Ahaz to ask God to reveal a Divine sign either in Sheol or in heaven (Isaiah 7:11). And the Hebrews came increasingly to believe that Yahweh was so powerful and just that His influence was felt throughout the entire universe—the sky, the earth, and Sheol (Psalm 139:7–10).

Further, they came increasingly to believe that Yahweh would redeem people's souls from even Sheol (Psalm 49:15). The belief in Sheol came to be transformed. The more the Hebrews thought of Yahweh as unsurpassably just and powerful, the more they came to see Sheol not as a meaningless, non-moral land of forgetfulness but as a land of ethical importance, in which rewards and punishments were administered. The Hebrews came to picture Yahweh as concerned not only with the Hebrew nation but also with the fate of individuals. It has been argued that when the book of Job was written (probably between the 6th and 5th centuries B.C.) the idea, or hope, of resurrection was in the air. Although most of Job's remarks about Sheol are negative and hopeless (for example, Job 7:9), he is presented as hoping for deliverance from Sheol (14:13–15; 19:25–27).

But as suggested earlier, such hints as there are about resurrection are few, and even they occur late. Two psalms at least appear to hint at an expectation of freedom from Sheol, Psalms 73:23–26 and 16:8–11. And the book of Daniel, as noted earlier, contains a fairly unambiguous reference to resurrection: "And many of those whose bodies lie dead and buried will rise up, some to everlasting life and some to shame and everlasting contempt" (12:2). Another generally accepted reference occurs in Isaiah 26:19: "Those who belong to God shall live again. Their bodies shall rise again! Those who dwell in the dust shall awake and sing for joy! For God's light of life will fall like dew upon them!"

Given that the Old Testament references to resurrection are extremely rare, and given that most of the Old Testament contains verses suggesting that the dead are without hope, it is hardly surprising that the Sadducees of Jesus' day rejected the belief in resurrection (Acts 23:8).

The point to seize here is that the voices of the Bible do not always speak in unison. In the matter of resurrection, for example, the Old Testament speaks with many voices. The concept of resurrection developed during the historical process of the creation of the Bible.

DO THE DIFFERENT TRANSLATIONS OF THE BIBLE REALLY MATTER?

Do different English versions of the Bible make significant changes in the wording of particular verses, or do they make only *grammatical* and *stylistic* changes (such as 'thou' being changed to 'you')? Different versions *often do* significantly alter the wording, depending on the particular interpretation that the translator or editor wants to place on the verse. We are not concerned here to decide whether one version is more accurate than another, or which translation is most reliable. But differences among translations do show that readers might not know for certain whether they are receiving the correct impression of a verse's meaning—whether they are properly understanding the original message—when they read a particular version or paraphrase of the Bible. Readers might also not know which versions and paraphrases allow them to understand better the intended meanings of the Bible, and which ones include translations that are most likely to be misunderstood.

Consider the following comparisons of *The Book* with the *King James Version* of the Bible. (Note that *The Book* is the Bible from which all our quotations throughout this book, unless otherwise indicated, are taken. With the exception of the following quotations, we have at all times made sure to use only those verses paraphrased in *The Book* that are essentially in agreement with reputable translations, such as the *Revised Standard Version*. The following comparisons are presented not to condone or condemn any particular paraphrase or version of the Bible, but rather only to illustrate how differences in wording among different paraphrases or versions sometimes can change one's perception of the meanings of certain verses.)

1. In Genesis 2:17, according to *The Book,* God warns Adam about eating from the fruit of the Tree of Knowledge: "If you eat its fruit you will be doomed to die." With that translation, the fact that Adam did not die on the day that he disobeyed God but that he did ultimately die at the age of 930 (Genesis 5:5) would not seem particularly contradictory. But the *King James Version* of Genesis 2:17 implies that God had said that Adam would indeed die on the very day that he ate the fruit: ". . . in the day that thou eatest thereof thou shalt surely die."

2. Exodus 34:14 in the *King James Version* reads: "For thou shalt worship no other god: for the Lord, whose name is Jealous, is a jealous God." The implication presented here is that the Lord exhibits jealousy. In *The Book,* the latter part of this verse reads simply that "he is a God who claims absolute loyalty and exclusive devotion", with no statement of what His "name" is.

3. *The Book*'s version of Deuteronomy 34:6 records that "no one knows the exact place" where Moses was buried. In the *King James Version,* however, the same sentence ends with

the phrase, "unto this day." This latter phrase lends evidence that the account of Moses' burial was most likely written many years after the time of Moses, traditionally considered the author of Deuteronomy.

4. The phrase, "that outlived Joshua", which appears at the end of Joshua 24:31 in the *King James Version*, is eliminated from *The Book*, which reads: "Israel obeyed the Lord throughout the lifetimes of Joshua and the other old men. . . ." That verse, in effect, removes an implication that Joshua was probably not the author of the book of Joshua, since he would logically not have known whether Israel obeyed the Lord throughout the lifetimes of men who *lived after he had died*.

5. The *King James Version* mentions "the five sons" of Michal (2 Samuel 21:8) while *The Book* version refers to "the five adopted sons." The *King James Version* seems to contradict 2 Samuel 6:23, which states that "Michal was childless throughout her life."

6. In 2 Kings 2:23–24, *The Book* describes this occurrence as the prophet Elisha was walking along the road to Bethel: ". . . a gang of young men from the city began mocking and making fun of him because of his bald head. He turned around and cursed them in the name of the Lord; and two female bears came out of the woods and tore forty-two of them." The *King James Version*, however, indicates that it was only "little children out of the city" who so mocked Elisha. The latter version makes the prophet's behavior seem particularly suspect and overharsh, while *The Book*, which refers not to "children" but rather to "a gang", in effect reduces that implication.

7. In Job 7:9, the *King James Version* states that "he that goeth down to the grave shall come up no more." That appears to be a direct contradiction to the New Testament notion shared by both *The Book* and *King James Version* that the return of the Messiah would be indicated by "a trumpet blast from the sky and all the Christians who have died will suddenly come alive" (*The Book*) or "shall be raised" (*King James Version*) (1 Corinthians 15:52). That verse seems also to contradict those instances where the Bible records certain people

being raised from the dead (for example, 2 Kings 4:32–36; John 11:38–44; Acts 26:23).

In *The Book's* version of Job 7:9, however, all those implications of contradictions are less obvious, the verse reading that "those who die shall go away forever"—not that they shall "never come up."

8. In Psalm 86:8, the sentence, "Among the gods there is none like unto thee, O Lord" (*King James Version*), becomes "Where among the heathen gods is there a god like you?" in *The Book*. Thus, the notion that God may be simply better than the other Gods—but that those Gods were believed to exist as well—is, in effect, diluted by the insertion of the word "heathen".

9. In Ecclesiastes 1:4, according to the *King James Version*, "One generation passeth away, and another generation cometh: but the earth abideth for ever." That translation of the verse seems to contradict the New Testament notion that when the Messiah returns, "the heavenly bodies will disappear in fire, the earth and everything on it will be burned up" (2 Peter 3:10). *The Book*, however, avoids any impression of a contradiction, saying in Ecclesiastes simply that "Generations come and go but it makes no difference. The sun rises and sets and hurries around to rise again." There, then, no claim is made that the Earth "abideth for ever".

10. In the *King James Version*, the author of Jeremiah 27:3 mistakenly refers to "Zedekiah king of Judah", whereas it is clear from the surrounding verses that Jehoiakim, the king of Judah, was the correct name of the person to whom the reference should have been made. In *The Book's* version of that verse neither Zedekiah nor Jehoiakim is mentioned, in effect removing the appearance of error.

11. Before deciding to follow Jesus, one of Jesus' disciples said to Jesus (according to *The Book*), "Sir, when my father is dead, then I will follow you." Jesus' reply was, "Follow me now! Let those who are spiritually dead care for their own dead." The *King James Version* of this same verse, however, gives no impression that the discussion dealt with the "spiritually" dead, but rather, in fact, that it dealt with the physically dead. Thus, according to the *King James Version*, the disciple

said, "suffer me first to go and bury my father," and Jesus replied, "Follow me; and let the dead bury their dead." *The Book*, with its "spiritually dead" reference, therefore tends to remove any impression that Jesus may have been encouraging the forsaking of the sacred duty of burying one's own father (Matthew 8:22).

12. In the Sermon on the Mount, Jesus, according to the *King James Version*, warns against cursing, saying that "whosoever shall say, Thou fool, shall be in danger of hell fire" (Matthew 5:22). Yet on at least two occasions Jesus is claimed to have referred to certain people as "Fools!" (Matthew 23:17) and "Blind fools!" (Luke 11:40). This apparent hypocrisy of Jesus is, however, not so obvious in *The Book* because there Jesus is recorded as having said in his Sermon on the Mount: "If you call your friend an idiot, you are in danger of being brought before the court. And if you curse him, you are in danger of the fires of hell." Thus, according to *The Book*'s version of Matthew 5:22, Jesus never directly prohibited the use of the word 'fool'.

13. In the *King James Version*, Jesus told his followers that "If any man come to me, and hate not his father, and mother, and wife, and children, and brethren, and sisters, yea, and his own life also, he cannot be my disciple" (Luke 14:26). *The Book*, however, does not include the unloving-sounding word, 'hate', and the verse states simply that Jesus expected his disciples to "love me far more than" they loved their family.

14. The phrase, "What have I to do with thee?" appears in the *King James Version* in John 2:4. Its harsh connotation seems to portray Jesus as rude to his mother: "Jesus saith to her, Woman, what have I to do with thee? mine hour is not yet come." In *The Book*, however, the same verse does not appear impolite: " 'I can't help you now,' he said. 'It isn't yet my time for miracles.' "

15. Acts 22:9, according to the *King James Version*, says that "they heard not the voice that spake to me." That verse appears to contradict Acts 9:7, which, describing the same incident, says that "they heard the sound of someone's voice." *The Book*'s version of Acts 22:9, however, states, "The men

with me . . . didn't understand what was said." Thus, with *The Book*'s reading, Acts 9:7 is not contradicted, because the people could still have heard the sound but simply not *understood* what it said.

16. According to 1 Timothy 6:10 in the *King James Version*, "the love of money is the root of all evil." *The Book*'s version of that verse, however, does not make such a generalization, saying instead that "the love of money is the first step toward all kinds of sin."

(For detailed footnotes identifying many of the other verses in *The Book* that are different from such translations as the *King James Version*, one may also want to consult *The Living Bible*, which contains the same text as *The Book*. Another work useful for making comparisons is *The Layman's Parallel New Testament* [Grand Rapids, Mich.: Zondervan Publishing House, 1970], which presents three versions, and one paraphrase, of the New Testament side by side: the *King James Version*, the *Revised Standard Version, The Amplified Version* [La Habra, Calif.: Lockman Foundation, 1958], and *The Living New Testament* [Wheaton, Ill.: Tyndale House, 1967].)

DOES AN AUTHENTIC BIBLE EXIST?

Is there any original copy of the Bible in existence? The claim, for instance, that any inconsistencies in the Bible are not contained in the Bible's original manuscript is a highly dubious contention and reflects a misconception, because *no original manuscript of any book of the Bible is known to exist.* No one has discovered even one copy of any original Biblical manuscript, often called 'original autographs'.

The Bible manuscripts which have survived are copies of copies of copies (and so on) made not by the original authors but by scribes. Many of these copies (apographs) vary in their texts. Without the benefit of printing presses or photocopiers, scribes made alterations, sometimes committing human error, sometimes making stylistic or grammatical changes, sometimes trying to harmonize conflicting passages or to clarify others, and sometimes expanding stories or adding new ones.

The story, for example, in John 8 in which Jesus forgives the adulteress appears only in later New Testament manuscripts. Similarly, the description in John 5:3–4 of angels disturbing the water at a pool is evidently a later insertion, since it does not appear in any earlier manuscripts. It was added, perhaps, to explain the "movement of the water" mentioned in John 5:7.

'Correctors' made further alterations to the scribes' work. Along with their changes, copies were subsequently copied by other scribes, and those copies were later copied, and so on. Thus, a complex web of altered texts was established. Anyone who claims that certain extant manuscripts may be errant, but that the original autographs were inerrant, is making, therefore, a claim for which no evidence can be found.

DO WE HAVE THE COMPLETE BIBLE?

Is the Bible complete? In the Old Testament several verses refer to other books of apparently equal authority as the Bible including *The Book of the Wars of Jehovah* (mentioned in Numbers 21:14), *The Book of Jashar* (Joshua 10:13), heroic ballads, and "the annals of King David" (1 Chronicles 27:24), none of which is found within the Bible.

Further, 1 Chronicles 29:29 states that "detailed biographies of King David" are written "in the history of Samuel the prophet, the history written by Nathan the prophet, and in the history written by the prophet Gad." The "rest of Solomon's biography", according to 2 Chronicles 9:29, is written "in the history of Nathan the prophet and in the prophecy of Ahijah the Shilonite, and . . . in the visions of Iddo the seer concerning Jeroboam the son of Nebat." 1 Kings 11:41 indicates that "the rest of what Solomon did and said" is written in "The book *The Acts of Solomon*." The "complete biography of Rehoboam" is said to have been recorded "in the histories written by Shemaiah the prophet and by Iddo the seer" (2 Chronicles 12:15). And according to 2 Chronicles 13:22, "the complete biography and speeches" of King Abijah of Judah are recorded in the prophet Iddo's History of Judah.

Still further, New Testament authors used the Greek translation of the Hebrew Old Testament (called the Septuagint), which included not only the books that Protestants today accept as Old Testament Scripture but also the following works: additions to Esther, additions to Daniel ('Prayer of

Azariah and the Song of the Three Young Men', 'History of Susanna', and 'Bel and the Dragon'), 1 Baruch, Letter of Jeremiah, Tobit, Judith, 1 Esdras (also known as either 2 Ezra or 3 Esdras), 2 Esdras, Ecclesiasticus (or Ben Sira or Wisdom of Jesus Son of Sirach), Wisdom of Solomon, Prayer of Manasseh, and I, II, III, and IV Maccabees.

Those additional works, sometimes referred to as Apocrypha, were accepted throughout the Greek and Latin world until at least the fourth century A.D., and most early Church Fathers treated them as inspired Scripture. In 1546, the Council of Trent decreed that they were all part of the Old Testament canon (except Prayer of Manasseh and 1 and 2 Esdras); and in 1672, at the Synod of Jerusalem, the canonical status of the books of Wisdom, Tobit, Bel and the Dragon, Susanna, Maccabees, and Ecclesiasticus was reaffirmed.

While not accepted as canonical among today's Protestant churches, most of those books are considered part of the Old Testament canon among Roman Catholic, Greek Orthodox, Armenian, and Ethiopian churches, as well as among Ethiopian Jews. (For further reading, refer to *The Oxford Annotated Apocrypha* [*Revised Standard Version*] [New York: Oxford University Press, 1965].)

People did not recognize as sacred the books of the Bible at the time they were originally written. There is no reason to assume that even the writers of these books had any notion that what they were writing would one day be included in a collection chosen by the Christian churches, and given the name 'Bible'. The books of the Bible acquired their sacred status only over a period of time. For example, the book of Esther became a part of the Bible mainly because it was traditionally read each year during the Hebrew festival of Purim; and the book of Psalms was the hymnbook of the Temple. Further, there was not complete agreement about which books should be accepted as part of the Biblical canon. Even after the Council of Jamnia (around A.D. 90), at which, supposedly, the Old Testament canon was finally fixed, many rabbinic scholars were still unwilling to accept Esther, Ecclesiastes, and the Song of Solomon as authoritative. Indeed, even today among many Jewish congregations, not all Old Testament books are regarded as equally authoritative, the first five books (the 'Five Books of Moses' or 'Torah') being regarded as far more authoritative than most of the others.

Great controversy also surrounded the canonization of New Testament books. For example, before the middle of the fourth century the status of such epistles as James, 2 Peter, Jude, and 2 and 3 John was still questionable, and only with great hesitation were those works accepted. Similarly, the book of Hebrews was generally accepted only in the west, and Revelation only in the east, and not until the late fourth century was their acceptance made firm. Conversely, books such as The Teaching of the Twelve Apostles, Barnabas, the Gospel of Peter, The Apocalypse of Peter, Acts of Paul, 1 Clement, and The Shepherd were valued by some of the early Church fathers, but were ultimately not canonized.

Unfortunately, many fundamentalists know almost nothing about the early history of the Christian church. They know the New Testament and they know something about the Protestant Reformation in sixteenth-century Europe, but they have very little idea of what happened in between. It comes as a shock to such fundamentalists to discover that *the Christian church lasted for its first 300 years without the Bible as we know it*. The New Testament in its present form did not exist. For the first 100 years or so, some of the books which now belong to the New Testament were still being written. They were not regarded as infallible or Divinely inspired. They were viewed rather as fundamentalists now view the writings of Jerry Falwell and Pat Robertson—valuable counsel by respected Christians, but human and fallible. (It is very noticeable that some New Testament writings are ad hoc, occasional pieces, written for very specific readers. For instance, they may name an individual in passing, without giving any further information about him.) Later, local churches began to collect some of these writings that were considered authoritative. Such a collection is called a 'canon'. There were rival canons which differed, though eventually some writings became recognized by virtually all Christians. The earliest exact reference to the 'complete' New Testament canon as we now know it was in the year 367, in a letter by Athanasius. This canon was formally accepted by a council at Rome in 382. It was still *not* regarded as Divinely inspired—that view arose later. Thus, the New Testament was produced by churches and traditions. (We strongly recommend anyone interested in this subject to read the book by Harry Gamble listed in the bibliography below.)

Even long after the New Testament had been firmly established, theologians sometimes claimed that some of its books should not be considered authoritative. Thus, during the sixteenth century, Martin Luther could adamantly condemn the Epistle of James as worthless, an "epistle of straw".

Fundamentalists who believe that everything in the Bible is infallible must presumably believe that those individuals, groups of Jews and Christians over the centuries, who decided what would be included in the Bible, were also infallible.

ARE THE BIBLE'S TEACHINGS UNIQUE?

Is Christianity and its Judaic basis original, unique, sharing essentially nothing with contemporary or preceding religions, cults, philosophies, mythologies, or superstitions of the ancient world, pagan cultures, or primitive cultures? The answer is definitely no, since many aspects of Judeo-Christian religious practice, principles, and traditions are found, with some variations, in many religions and cultures that pre-date the Bible. The point here is not to discredit any religious belief by pointing out its similarity to beliefs in other religions. Rather, the point is to show that the beliefs and rituals in Biblical times were largely shared by different cultures; thus, the view that one can be certain that Jews and Christians were uniquely privy to Divine truth is a misconception.

Almost any book on ancient religions, primitive religions, mythology, anthropology, comparative religions, or the history of religion will reveal categorically proven examples of many of the following *pre-Biblical* rituals, traditions, and beliefs. (For a list of some of those works, please consult the bibliography at the end of this book.)

    1. Ceremonies of purification with water (like baptism).

    2. Prohibitions and taboos.

3. Fasting.

4. Sacrifices and vicarious atonement through the death of a God.

5. Immortality.

6. Union of a God and a virgin.

7. Trinities.

8. Annual sacrifices of criminal (like Barabbas, Mark 15:6–12).

9. The mother Mary (Myrrha, Maya, Maia, and Maritala, for example, were the mothers of Adonis, the Buddha, Hermes, and Krishna, respectively).

10. A place above for good people who die (like heaven) and a hell of fire with monsters whose heads are crowned with gold.

11. An apocalypse.

12. Creation from water.

13. An original earthly paradise (like Eden) occupied by mortals (like Adam and Eve) who dwelt with the Gods (like Yahweh), and containing rivers that watered the earth flowing from it.

14. The first man falling from a God's favor by doing something forbidden, having been tempted by some evil animal.

15. Catastrophic floods in which the whole race is exterminated because man has become hopelessly wicked, in which the survivors are succored by a bird that reveals its mission with some object (like an olive leaf), in which an ark rests atop a mountain (for example, Babylonian ark on Mt. Nisir, Hindu ark on Mt. Himalaya, Greek ark on Mt. Parnassus), and in which the hero is warned by a God.

16. A man being swallowed by a 'fish' and then spat out alive (for example, Hercules, who was swallowed by a whale at the same place as Jonah, in Joppa, and for the same length of time, three days).

17. Prodigious ages of patriarchs.

18. Separate castes or hierarchies of religious leaders or priests.

19. Certain people who have special favor with the Gods so that they can influence them: priests as law-givers, as

sacrifice-makers, as evil-spell-dispellers, as dream-interpreters, as anointers, as miracle-workers, as God's spokespersons, and as healers who can exorcise evil spirits.

20. Miracles as proofs of power of Divine messengers.

21. Gods who give success in war and who can be influenced to favor people.

22. Failures and natural disasters as indications of the Gods' divine displeasure with the people.

23. Unclean spirits possessing people.

24. A foe of the Gods, accuser of the good, and tempter of men to evil (like devils and demons).

25. Covenants between people and their Gods.

26. Certain words (in forms of chants, hymns, poems, songs, prayers) and acts that please or displease the Gods.

27. Sacred objects, symbols (such as the cross, halo, rosary, the scapular, candles, holy water, incense), and rods as instruments of miracle- making.

28. Special holy days (holidays), including, for example, a festival of thanksgiving for autumn harvest (see Deuteronomy 16).

29. Death, and then resurrection, of a saviour in three days (such as of Attis in cult of Cybele).

30. December 25 as significant date (for example, the birthday of the Unconquered Sun, a popular festival of the Mithraic cult during the later Roman Empire).

Apparently, then, the pagans even of pre-Biblical times had many religious concepts analogous to those of the Hebrews and Christians.

DOES THE BIBLE CONTAIN MORE THAN ONE VIEW OF GOD?

Did the people of the Bible have a clear notion of exactly who God is? However one answers that question, it is clear that Old Testament writers had different conceptions of how many Gods there were and which one, or ones, could be considered real. There are many references, especially in the early books of the Bible, suggesting that the Israelites conceived of God as being *their* God, but not the God of other peoples. Hence, the Ten Commandments did not say, "I am

Jehovah, the *only* God," but rather "I am Jehovah *your* God who liberated *you* from your slavery in Egypt" (Exodus 20:2; our italics). Similarly, the second commandment did not say that there were no other Gods, but only that His people, the Israelites, "may worship no other god than me." And in Exodus 34:14, "For you must worship no *other* gods, but only Jehovah, for he is *a* God who claims absolute loyalty and exclusive devotion" (our italics). Likewise in Psalms, "Those choosing other gods shall all be filled with sorrow; I will not . . . even speak the names of their gods" (16:4), and *"You must never worship any other god"* (81:9). In other words, Yahweh was considered "the God of Israel". (Note: the name 'Jehovah', which appears in some versions of the Bible, is simply a misreading of 'Yahweh'.)

In several instances the Biblical God Himself appears to have accepted the reality of the existence of other Gods. For example, in Exodus 12:12, Yahweh reportedly threatened to "pass through the land of Egypt tonight" and "execute judgment upon all the gods of Egypt." Likewise, the prophet Zephaniah proclaimed God's intent to "starve out all those gods of foreign powers" so that "everyone shall worship . . . the Lord Almighty, God of Israel" (Zephaniah 2:11). It is noteworthy that among the many times that other "gods" are referred to in the Bible, usually no indication is given that those Gods were perceived as not being real or even as not able to perform miracles. Often there is only the indication that God would punish the people who worship them. Note further that when the psalmist wrote that "you [the Lord] are far greater than these other gods" (97:9), he did not clearly indicate that he thought that the "Lord" was necessarily the *only* God.

CONCLUSION

The Bible is a work rich in meaning and ambiguity. As such, it may easily be misunderstood, especially if it is viewed as easily comprehensible and *directly* applicable to all aspects of everyday life. Many people who take that approach, particularly fundamentalists, risk not being able to appreciate the degree to which even the most sincere people can seriously misconstrue the meaning of many parts of the Bible. Indeed, as will be demonstrated in the next chapter, many of the most devout and learned Christians of the past sometimes regarded the Bible as endorsing their own human frailties and shortcomings, including prejudice and intolerance.

CHAPTER 9

ANTI-SEMITISM AND THE CONTROVERSIAL

USE OF THE BIBLE

One of the potential hazards in fundamentalism is that people who hold the doctrine of Biblical inerrancy may not be able to appreciate the degree to which certain verses in the Bible can be exploited to promote ethnic or religious intolerance. Since one of the most poignant examples of how easily the Bible can be misused for such purposes is the historical connection between the New Testament and anti-Semitism, it is on that subject that this chapter will focus. (Please note that this discussion is not in any way intended to imply that fundamentalists are anti-Semitic. Indeed, the great majority of American fundamentalists today hold a high regard for their Jewish brethren; and anti-Semitism is, in fact, probably not as much a problem among fundamentalists as it is among some other groups. Nonetheless, a discussion of 'Christian' anti-Semitism is important because the issue illustrates the profound danger inherent in an unquestioning acceptance of any Biblical verses.)

The New Testament has been used by some of the most revered Christians in history to support anti-Jewish hatred. The New Testament does not say anywhere that the Jews should be hated, ostracized, or otherwise persecuted. And the Church fathers, were, for the most part, sincere men whose selfless concern for their flock was both admirable and inspiring. Sadly, though, the New Testament has, by its apparent criticisms of the Jewish rejection of Jesus, often been taken to justify hatred toward Jews. Although many Christians have ignored the Jewishness of the New Testament, they have throughout history placed special emphasis upon its anti-Jewish verses and its teachings about the damnation of those who do not accept Jesus' Messiahship. Those verses and teachings, perhaps inevitably, have contributed to an enormous amount of anti-Semitism. Influenced by certain verses, many of the leading lights of the Church have expressed grotesque anti-Semitism and condoned or positively endorsed mistreatment of Jews. Indeed, it is only very recently that churches have been trying to condemn the anti-Semitism that has long been a part of their past. (Note that we are *not* claiming that all or even most anti-Semitic Christians throughout history regarded *every* Biblical verse as inerrant. Nor are we claiming that the treatment of the New Testament is the *only* historical factor for 'Christian' anti-Semitism. Instead, our claim is simply that much anti-Semitism has been due to treating certain New Testament verses as beyond question and without historical sensitivity.)

Why has the New Testament sometimes been a tool of anti-Jewish oppression? Perhaps a principal reason is the insistence that the Bible is largely unquestionable in its beliefs and attitudes. When taken as absolutely true, even by the most sincere religious persons, some verses in the Bible can be used as tools for the most vicious purposes. Consequently, people who have far less knowledge of the Bible than many of the Church fathers and other religious leaders should be wary of investing Biblical verses with dogmatic certitude.

The first part of this chapter will present three major points:

1. That the life of the Biblical Jesus was very much a Jewish one, played out almost entirely within the Jewish community, neither opposed to nor separated from Judaism. Thus, using the Bible to support hostility to Jews contradicts both the Jewishness of Jesus and the Judaic foundation of Christianity.

2. That, while the New Testament has no injunctions to hate or harm Jews, its theology at times so strongly condemns anyone who rejects Christ that it has inspired some forms of anti-Semitism.

3. And, likewise, that the tendency of the New Testament writers to portray some, or all, Jewish people in Jesus' time as guilty of the Crucifixion, has inspired anti-Semitism.

The last part of this chapter will present examples of the systematic way in which Christian leaders have encouraged anti-Semitism and their followers have persecuted Jews.

THE JEWISHNESS OF THE NEW TESTAMENT

Does the New Testament condone hatred of Jews and Judaism? It can easily so appear, especially by the unquestioning believer, but really the New Testament often esteems Judaism.

In his Sermon on the Mount, Jesus categorically states, "Don't misunderstand why I have come—it isn't to cancel the laws of Moses and the warnings of the prophets. No, I came to fulfill them, and to make them all come true. With all earnestness I have I say: Every law in the Book [Old Testament] will continue until its purpose is achieved . . ." (Matthew 5:17–18). Jesus complains about the hypocrisy of the Jews in his community, especially the Pharisees. Thus, his complaint is only that they are not behaving *according to the original Jewish laws* as they should. He tells "some Pharisees and other Jewish leaders" the following:

> . . . Why do your traditions violate the direct commandments of God? For instance, God's law [i.e., the law of Moses] is "Honor your father and mother; anyone who reviles his parents must die." But you say, "Even if your parents are in need, you may give their support money to the church instead." And so, by your man-made rule, you nullify the direct command of God to honor and care for your parents. You hypocrites! (Matthew 15:3–7)

There is certainly nothing new about debates within Judaism, which debated everything from written law to oral tradition. (It must be understood that what is frequently perceived as anti-Jewish sentiment in the New Testament is often merely inner conflict among different Jewish groups. Pharisees, Sadducees, Zealots, the Qumran community, baptist movements, assimilationists, and fanatics, were all divisions among the Jews in Jesus' world.) Even in his criticism, Jesus cites Jewish prophecy: "Well did Isaiah prophesy to you, 'These people say they honor me, but their hearts are far away. Their worship is worthless, for they teach their man-made laws instead of those from God' " (Matthew 15:8–9;

similarly Mark 7:6–8). Arguing about things like which prayers are worthwhile and which are not was no more than a typical Jewish debate. Later, when Jesus again complains about hypocrisy, he criticizes "these Jewish leaders and these Pharisees" for "making up so many laws", acting as though they were Moses: "It may be all right to do what they say, but above anything else, *don't follow their example*" (Matthew 23:2–3). Again, his basic criticism is of the things that they have *appended* to the original laws; he still wants the original laws to be followed, though humanely interpreted. He indicates that he expects people to behave better than the Pharisaic Jews but not necessarily better than the laws they are supposed to be following: ". . . unless your goodness is greater than that of the Pharisees and other Jewish leaders, you can't get into the Kingdom of Heaven at all!" (Matthew 5:20). Indeed, when certain Jews criticize Jesus and his disciples for doing work on the Sabbath (harvesting grain when hungry and healing people [Mark 2:23–24; 3:1–6; Matthew 12:1–14; Luke 6:1–11]), Jesus does not dismiss their claims, but defends himself on the basis of the value and use of the Jewish Sabbath and uses Old Testament examples:

> Is it all right to do kind deeds on Sabbath days? Or is this a day for doing harm? Is it a day to save lives or to destroy them? (Mark 3:4; similarly Matthew 12:11–12; Luke 6:9)

> Didn't you ever hear about the time King David and his companions were hungry, and he went into the house of God—Abiathar was High Priest then—and they ate the special bread only priests were allowed to eat? That was against the law too. But the Sabbath was made to benefit man, and not man to benefit the Sabbath. (Mark 2:25–26; similarly Matthew 12:3–7; Luke 6:3–5)

Even the Biblical Jesus' claim to Messiahship was quite Jewish and was taken to be based on the Old Testament prophecies. That is why, in the Gospel of Matthew in particular, extensive references are made to the fulfillment of Old Testament verses of Messianic prophecy. The Gospel writers, especially of the Synoptics (the first three Gospels), made every effort to show that virtually every aspect of Jesus' life and teachings—his Virgin Birth, his birth in Bethlehem (the city of David), his baptism, his Crucifixion, his Resurrection, et cetera—were all fulfillments of prophecies found in distinct Old Testament verses.

Jesus therefore did not claim to be seeking to establish a religion separate from Judaism. There is even some indication that Jesus came primarily if not only for the Jews. When a Canaanite woman pleaded for Jesus' help, he told her, "I was sent to help the Jews—the lost sheep of Israel—not the Gentiles" (Matthew 15:24). Jesus also told his disciples, "Don't go to the Gentiles or the Samaritans, but only to the people of Israel—God's lost sheep" (Matthew 10:5–6).

Nor does the New Testament show that after Jesus' death early church leaders/apostles intended Christianity to be a religion separate from Judaism. Paul did not stop attending the Temple; indeed he used it for his gentile converts (Acts 21:28–29), hardly the thing to do if one is leaving the Jewish religion. At the Jewish Council, Paul proclaimed proudly that "I am a Pharisee, as were all my ancestors!" questioning why the council would doubt his Jewishness simply because he believed in the resurrection of the dead (Acts 23:6). Indeed, "Some of the Jewish leaders jumped up to argue that Paul was all right" (Acts 23:9), "for the Sadducees say there is no resurrection or angels or even eternal spirit within us, *but the Pharisees believe in all of these*" (our italics; Acts 23:8). Later, when accused of being "a ringleader of the sect known as the Nazarenes" and of inciting Jews to rebel against the Roman government (Acts 24:5), Paul objected: "You can quickly discover that it was no more than twelve days ago that I arrived in Jerusalem to worship at the Temple, and you will discover that I have never incited a riot in any synagogue or on the streets of any city; . . . I believe in the way of salvation, which they [his accusers] refer to as a sect; I follow that system of serving the God of our ancestors; I firmly believe in the Jewish law and everything written in the books of prophecy; . . ." (Acts 24:11–14.) At another trial, Paul repeated his denial of all charges: "I have not opposed the Jewish laws or desecrated the Temple or rebelled against the Roman government" (Acts 25:8).

In gaining Gentile converts to Christian Judaism, Paul wished to define Judaism in such a way that a Gentile convert could be a Jew without undergoing circumcision: "No, a real Jew is anyone whose heart is right with God. For God is not looking for those who cut their bodies in actual body circumcision, but he is looking for those with changed hearts and minds" (Romans 2:29). He also emphasized that even though faith in Jesus was required, it did not mean that God's laws were no longer needed. "Just the opposite!" he said, "In fact, only when we trust Jesus can we truly obey Him" (Romans 3:31). (Or, in the *Revised Standard Version:* "On the contrary, we uphold the law.") Even Jesus' brother James and the elders of the Jerusalem church showed concern about possibly offending the "many thousands of Jews" who belonged to the Christian movement. To allay any impression that Paul was opposed to the laws of Moses and the Jewish customs, the church elders instructed Paul to "Go . . . to the Temple and have your head shaved. . . . Then everyone will know that you approve of this custom for the Hebrew Christians and that you yourself obey the Jewish laws and are in line with our thinking in these matters." Paul agreed to their request (Acts 21:20–26).*

INTOLERANCE IN THE NEW TESTAMENT

It is the *theology* of the New Testament that has sometimes been used as a 'reason' to hate Jews. Parts of the New Testament proclaim that one must have faith in Jesus Christ to enter the kingdom of heaven. Faith in Jesus—and not simply

---

*Our discussion of Paul's attitude toward Jewish laws is not intended to deny that the New Testament appears occasionally to contain conflicting pictures of the degree to which Paul valued certain laws. For example, Luke, the author of Acts, who wanted to minimize the divisions within the early Christian movement, represented Paul as circumcising Timothy out of respect for the feelings of some Jews (Acts 16:3), whereas Paul, the author of Galatians described himself as opposed to circumcising gentile converts, regardless of resistance (Galatians 2:1–5, 5:11–12). The key point however is that, even though Luke might have represented the early Christian movement as more harmonious in the matter of obedience to Jewish laws than it was, the Book of Acts testifies to its author's sympathy for those people (including Paul) who conceived of Christianity as a further development of Judaism instead of as a separate religion. Although Paul did not think that obedience to law could gain people salvation, which required faith in Jesus, he upheld God's laws. Indeed, he believed that only by trusting Jesus could people naturally want to follow God's laws (Romans 3:31).

the laws of Judaism—was the way. Said Paul: "The old way, trying to be saved by keeping the Ten Commandments, ends in death; in the new way, the Holy Spirit gives them life" (2 Corinthians 3:6). Since "the old way" is the way of unChristianized Jews, holding that it "ends in death" is not a compliment for the religion of any people. Further, Paul's suggestion that believers in Jesus were in fact the "real" people of God (Galatians 4:22–31; 6:16), and that the Jewish "branches", lacking faith, were "broken off" by God (Romans 11:20) further belittled the value of Judaism. It must though be mentioned, in fairness to Paul, that he never taught hatred of unChristianized Jews. Indeed, he maintained that Christianized Jews were no better than unconverted Jews since all people are sinners (Romans 3:9–12). Thus, if Paul was negative toward unconverted Jews, he was equally negative to anyone else who intentionally rejected Jesus' Messiahship. Paul's intolerance for unChristianized Judaism was, therefore, theological, not ethnic.

According to his Epistle to the Romans (chapters 9–11), Paul believed that Jewish rejection of Christ was planned by God to spread Christianity among the Gentiles. He expected that Jews would convert increasingly to Christianity after the conversion of Gentiles. For him Judaism was like a teacher, leading people to the One True Faith—Christianity (Galatians 3:23). Paul's theology, in which unconverted Judaism was seen largely as only a steppingstone to Christianity, depreciated the integrity of Judaism. Although Paul opposed persecution of unconverted Jews (1 Corinthians 10:32–33) and regarded them as "beloved of God" (Romans 11:28), his theology condemned unconverted *Judaism*.

Some other parts of the New Testament condemn the rejection of Jesus' Messiahship with such finality that they have promoted the belief that unconverted Jews are wicked, damned, even Satanic. Although those are harsh words, they honestly reflect the theology in the most dogmatic parts of the Bible, where people are judged largely if not principally by their capacity to hold uncritically certain beliefs about Jesus.

The Gospels sometimes treat the rejection of Jesus' Messiahship as a perversion of God's will and a refusal to see and acknowledge the Light. Accordingly, disbelief in Jesus is damned in Matthew 10:33 and equated with attempting to thwart his will in Matthew 12:30. In Mark 16:16 also disbelief is condemned. The Gospel of John, though, more than any other Gospel, equates disbelief in Jesus with utter depravity. There rejection of Jesus is unconditionally condemned (3:18) on the ground that belief in Jesus is the only way to salvation (14:6). Disbelief in Jesus is equated with rejection of the Light, of Love, and of God. The Gospel of John, with its categorical condemnation of disbelief in Jesus, is an extremely theologically intolerant document.

Accordingly, John attributes the following remark to Jesus:

> There is no eternal doom awaiting those who trust him to save them. But those who don't trust him have already been tried and condemned for not believing in the only Son of God. Their sentence is based on this fact: that the Light from heaven came into the world, but they loved the darkness more than the Light, for their deeds were evil. They hated the heavenly Light because they wanted to sin in the darkness. (John 3:18–20)

Before that comment John notes, "Even in his own land and among his own people, the Jews, he was not accepted. Only a few would welcome and receive him. But to all who received him, he gave the right to become children of God" (John 1:11–12). Later, when some Jewish people who were speaking to Jesus said that they were descendants of their father Abraham, Jesus, according to the Fourth Gospel, replied:

> No! . . . for if he were [your father], you would follow his good example. . . . For you are the children of your father the devil and you love to do the evil things he does. He was a murderer from the beginning and a hater of truth—there is not an iota of truth in him. When he lies, it is perfectly normal; for he is the father of liars. (John 8:39–44)

Perhaps John was not condemning Jews as an ethnic group but was condemning only those Jews who contradicted, and ultimately rejected, Jesus. John, however, appears to equate the rejection of Jesus' Messiahship with Satanism. It is, therefore, largely because of the uncritical acceptance of certain interpretations of the Gospel of John that Jews have been labelled Satanic. Some of the historical consequences of that label will be described later in this chapter.

WHO IS TO BLAME FOR THE CRUCIFIXION?

The Gospel narrative of Jesus' crucifixion is so written that it fixes blame entirely, or almost entirely, on Jews or a number of Jewish leaders. Intentionally or not, that ascription of blame has inevitably led to prejudice against Jews.

For the most part, the Gospels do not portray all Jews as being guilty of crucifying Jesus. Indeed, the Synoptic Gospels (Matthew, Mark and Luke) usually portray only certain Jewish leaders of Jesus' day as directly involved. Thus, in Matthew 26, the conspirators against Jesus are represented as Caiaphus (the High Priest), as well as the chief priests and other Jewish officials, but not the Jewish people generally. For Jesus had to be arrested secretly and not during the festival (Passover) to avoid inciting the people to riot (Matthew 26:5). Thus, there is a clear distinction made between particular Jews and the Jewish people. Mark also blames the chief priests particularly rather than the Jews generally for the Crucifixion: ". . . the chief priests and other Jewish leaders . . . began planning how best to get rid of him. Their problem was their fear of riots because the people were so enthusiastic about Jesus' teaching" (Mark 11:18). "The Jewish leaders wanted to arrest him. . . . But they were afraid to touch him for fear of a mob" (Mark 12:12). Luke agrees with Mark, as evidenced by Luke 19:47–48; 20:19; and 22:2.

In Matthew 27, the story is told that "the chief priests and Jewish leaders met again to discuss how to induce the Roman government to sentence Jesus to death" (27:1) and then "they sent him in chains to Pilate, the Roman governor" (27:2). Later, "crowds" gathered around Pilate's house (27:17), and "the chief priests and Jewish officials persuaded the crowds to ask for . . . Jesus' death." Then, Matthew alleges that this statement was made by the crowd: "His blood be on us and on our children" (Matthew 27:25). Even if someone accepted that extraordinary self-accusation as historical, and the peculiar justice of condemning people's descendants for their ancestors' sins, that statement certainly did not represent *all* the

Jews in the entire world. Further, if there was an implication that even all the Jews in the town were aware of their alleged crime and committed it willingly, that notion is laid to rest in Peter's epistles. In his announcement on the question of Jewish guilt, addressed to "men of Israel" (Acts 2:22), he concluded with the remark: "Dear brothers, I realize that what you did to Jesus was done in ignorance; and the same can be said of your leaders" (Acts 3:17). And when Peter addressed the Jewish Council, the High Priest showed no such willingness to have "the blame for this man's death" brought "on us" (Acts 5:28).

Even fundamentalist Jerry Falwell does not accept fully the notion of Jewish blame implied in Matthew 27:25. Falwell maintains that no one was any more, or less, to blame, since Jesus intended to be crucified. Says Falwell, "I do not think anyone was responsible for the murder of Christ because I don't think Christ was murdered. . . . I believe that he willingly laid down his life. . . . All persons in every age must share in the blame for Christ's death. . . . [Since we] are all sinners, Jews and Gentiles, every human being in every age contributed to his crucifixion." (*Jerry Falwell and The Jews*, by Merrill Simon [New York: Jonathan David, 1984], p.23.) Nonetheless, Matthew's statement has provided the fuel for an enormous amount of anti-Semitism. It should also be understood that although the Gospels of Matthew, Mark, and Luke imply that only a small number of the Jews of Jesus' time were involved in the Crucifixion—and thus, by inference, that not all Jews should be blamed—the New Testament stories, nonetheless, have throughout history inspired much anti-Semitism.

It is the Gospel of John, however, that has intensified the accusations of blame by his oft-used ambiguous phrase, "the Jews" (as in, for example, John 5:10, 16; 7:1; 9:22; 10:19, 24, 31, 33; 18:36, 38; 19:7, 12, 14, 15; in the *Revised Standard Version*, *King James Version*, et cetera—but not *The Book*), in place of the more descriptive "Jewish leaders" or similar designations made in the Synoptic Gospels. By comparing the accounts in the Synoptics, it is apparent that where John refers to "the Jews" he is usually speaking of the Jewish leaders.

Note that, unlike most major Bible versions including the *Revised Standard* and *King James* versions, *The Book* paraphrase has usually changed John's "the Jews" to "the Jewish leaders". As a whole, however, John's Gospel never gives any clear indication that John himself intended "the Jews" to mean "Jewish leaders". Further, John's Gospel contains the most intolerant remarks of any of the Gospels (see previous section on "theology").

Unfortunately, throughout history those who have sought an excuse to hate Jews have often used John's Gospel especially in their defense. But while some may well suggest that John himself was anti-Semitic, there is nonetheless no statement, even by him, that Jews should be hated. John's theological intolerance, however, does condemn unconverted Jews and does—on some plausible readings—label such Jews Satanic. While the New Testament nowhere explicitly endorses anti-Semitism, its treatment of the Crucifixion and its intolerant theology have promoted beliefs and attitudes that have led, almost inevitably, to the hatred and persecution of millions of people.

CHRISTIAN ANTI-SEMITISM IN HISTORY

Have Christian leaders condoned anti-Semitic behavior? As Jerry Falwell acknowledges, "it is tragically true that untold multitudes of Jews have been slaughtered throughout history in the name of Christianity" (*Jerry Falwell and The Jews*, p.24). There is ample evidence. This section will present a brief account of some of the most atrocious sentiments ever expressed about a group of human beings. And what is more tragic, they are expressed in the name of the perfect, all-loving God. They are some of the most despicable examples of hatred ever expressed, yet they emanated from Christian leaders who were well-versed in knowledge of the Bible. Those leaders misinterpreted the all-too-human expressions of hostility (just mentioned in the previous section of this chapter) found occasionally in the Gospels aimed at particular Jews and Jewish groups of Biblical times, and they utterly disregarded the parts of the Bible that demand love of one's neighbor and one's enemies.

From its beginnings, the rift between Christianity and Judaism increased as the new religion became predominantly Gentile and no longer merely a Christianized Judaism. Hostility to Jews increased after A.D. 313, when the Christian Emperor Constantine issued the Edict of Milan, which assured tolerance for all Christians throughout the Empire, but did not in practice assure religious freedom for Jews. For on October 18, 315, the first law passed by the triumphant Christians required "the consigning to the flames of Jews who acted to prevent other Jews from becoming Christians and of Christians who joined the 'evil sect' of Judaism" (James Parkes, *Judaism and Christianity* [Chicago: University of Chicago Press, 1948], p.119; cited in A. Roy Eckardt, *Your People, My People* [New York: New York Times Book Co., 1974], p.18).

It was during the fourth century that the church became increasingly dogmatic and intolerant of religious diversity. During that century Arius (A.D. 256–336), a Greek ecclesiastic at Alexandria, held that God the Father and God the Son are distinct, the latter having been created out of nothing. The Council of Nicaea in A.D. 325 hereticated the Arian position for rejecting the belief that God and Christ are co-eternal and consubstantial (of the same substance). The Council's decision in effect precluded differing views concerning Jesus and impeded the free use of the mind in matters Christian. As Christians became increasingly concerned with defining orthodoxy, they became increasingly hostile to religious diversity.

The church's hostility to religious diversity left Jews no place to go in the Empire to practice their religion without stigma. Typical of the fourth century were the views of St. John Chrysostom (345?–407), who has the dubious distinction of being one of the most anti-Jewish bigots who ever lived. Note that 'the Golden-Mouthed' saint is considered one of the greatest of the Church Fathers, hugely admired by Protestants and Catholics alike. John Henry Newman wrote: "A bright cheerful gentle soul, a sensitive heart, a temperament open to emotion and impulse; and all this elevated, refined, transformed by the touch of heaven,—such was St. John Chrysostom" (*Historical Sketches*, II, 234). That gentle soul hated with every drop of his blood millions of Jews and never tired of heaping contempt on them. Historian Malcolm Hay outlines the kinds of remarks made by Chrysostom that helped set the pattern for anti-Jewish hatred in Christendom:

> "The synagogue," he said, "is worse than a brothel . . . it is the den of scoundrels and the repair of wild beasts . . . The temple of demons devoted to idolatrous cults . . . the refuge of brigands and debauchees, and the cavern of devils."
>
> The synagogue, he told his congregations in another sermon, was "a criminal assembly of Jews . . . a place of meeting for the assassins of Christ . . . a house worse than a drinking shop . . . a den of thieves; a house of ill fame, a dwelling of iniquity, the refuge of devils, a gulf and abyss of perdition." And he concluded, exhausted at length by his eloquence: "Whatever name even more horrible could be found, will never be worse than the synagogue deserves." . . .
>
> In reply to some Christians who had maintained the Jewish synagogues might be entitled to respect because in them were kept the writings of Moses and the prophets, St. John Chrysostom answered: Not at all! This was a reason for hating them more, because they use these books, but willfully misunderstand their meaning. "As for me, I hate the synagogue . . . I hate the Jews for the same reason."
>
> It is not difficult to imagine the effect such sermons must have had upon congregations. . . . Not only every synagogue, Chrysostom told them, but every Jew, was a temple of the devil. "I would say the same things about their souls." And he said a great deal more. It was unfit, he proclaimed, for Christians to associate with a people who had fallen into a condition lower than the vilest animals. "Debauchery and drunkenness had brought them to the level of the lusty goat and the pig. They know only one thing, to satisfy their stomachs, to get drunk, to kill and beat each other up like stage villains and coachmen" (Malcolm Hay, *Europe and The Jews* [Boston: Beacon Press, 1960], pp.28–29)

St. Chrysostom flatly contradicted Peter (in Acts 5:28–33, in which the Jewish priests denied and resented charges that they had taken part in the Crucifixion), maintaining that "the Jews . . . erred not ignorantly but with full knowledge" (Homily viii, 'On the Gospel of St. John'). Chrysostom considered all Jews guilty of killing Christ and deserving of eternal servitude for their unpardonable crime. He went so far as to say that on Judgment Day God will say to any Christian who has ever talked with a Jew: "Depart from me, because you have had intercourse with murderers" (St. John Chrysostom, *Homilies Against the Jews*, 6.2, 7.1, cited in E.H. Flannery, *The Anguish of Jesus* [New York: Macmillan, 1965], pp.47–49).

Chrysostom has another equally dubious distinction— that of being the first Christian preacher to apply the word 'deicide' to the Jewish nation. In accordance with his view of Jews he believed that every tragedy and misfortune besetting Jews after the death of Jesus was a Divine punishment. (This viewpoint, which would become well-accepted, obviously disregarded the fact that Jews were not the only peoples to suffer; indeed the Middle Ages saw a long period of plagues and wars in which everyone, Jew and Gentile alike, suffered greatly.) He wrote: "Your situation, O Jewish people, becomes more and more disastrous, and one cannot see showing on your foreheads the slightest ray of hope." That is the logic of Hitler's crematoria. Thus, in his sermon, 'Sixth Homily Against the Jews', Chrysostom declared that if God did not want people to harm Jews, he would not allow them to do so. If St. Chrysostom were Divinely transplanted into the twentieth century, he would doubtless wax eloquent in declaring the Divine purpose behind Auschwitz, Maidenek, Dubno, and Treblinka. Consider now some other enormously influential Christians.

St. Athanasius (293?–373), a Greek Father of the Church who was known as 'Father of Orthodoxy', told people that "the Jews were no longer the people of God, but rulers of Sodom and Gomorrah" (Letter X [A.D. 338]). In his *Treatise On The Incarnation* (40, 7) he asked: "What is left unfulfilled, that they [the Jews] should now be allowed to disbelieve with impunity?"

St. Ambrose (340?–397), a bishop of Milan and a Father of the Church, told his congregations that the Jewish synagogue was "a house of impiety, a receptacle of folly, which God himself has condemned." Not surprisingly, some of Ambrose's followers set fire to a synagogue. Instead of condemning the arson, the good saint said: "I declare that I set fire to the synagogue, or at least that I ordered those who did it, that there might not be a place where Christ was denied. If it be objected to me that I did not set the synagogue on fire here, I answer it began to be burnt by the judgement of God" (Letter XI, to the Emperor Theodosius). He told Emperor Theodosius that the arsonists should not be punished because there was nothing of any value in the synagogue. When the Jews complained about the crime to the Emperor, Ambrose protested that Jews should not be testifying in a court of law, because they were liars. Said he: "Into what calumnies will they not break out, who, by false witness, calumniated even Christ!" (Cited in Hay's *Europe and The Jews*, pp. 25–26).

When St. Simeon Stylites (390?–459) discovered that the Emperor had tried to protect the synagogues from mobs, the saint asked the Emperor to revoke his orders for punishing the vandals. Stylites achieved distinction by living the last thirty-six years of his life on top of a pillar about fifty or sixty feet high, from which he, according to historian G.F. Abbot (*Israel In Europe*), gave up "all worldly luxuries except Jew-hatred" (Cited in Hay's *Europe and The Jews*, p. 26).

St. Gregory of Nyssa (331?–396?), one of the Fathers of the Eastern Church, described the Jewish people thus:

> Slayers of the Lord, murderers of the prophets, adversaries of God, haters of God, men who show contempt for the law, foes of grace, enemies of their father's faith, advocates of the devil, brood of vipers, slanderers, scoffers, men whose minds are in darkness, leaven of the Pharisees, assembly of demons, sinners, wicked men, stoners, and haters of righteousness. (St. Gregory, 'Oratio in Christi; resurrectionem,' p.685)

St. Augustine (354–430), another Church Father, considered one of the most influential and intelligent Christian theologians of all time, held that "The Jews, against whom the blood of Jesus Christ calls out, although they ought not to be killed . . . yet as wanderers must they remain upon the earth, until their countenance be filled with shame and they seek the name of Jesus Christ the Lord" (St. Augustine, *Commentary to Psalm 50; Contra Faustus 12:10*).

St. Augustine is widely held to have been the best Christian theologian until St. Thomas Aquinas (1225?–1274), who argued that Jewish guilt for the Crucifixion demanded their perpetual servitude (Hay's *Europe and The Jews*, p.27).

Aquinas's view was shared by Pope Innocent III (1161–1216), whom the *Catholic Encyclopedia* once described as "one of the greatest Popes of the Middle Ages, . . . whose politico-ecclesiastical achievements brought the papacy to the zenith of its power."

Results of Christians' Interpretation of the Bible's Views about Jews

The attitudes of the most influential Christians often had horrible consequences for the Jewish people. Writes Malcolm Hay:

> Under Christian rule they [the Jews] had hardly any rights. They were prohibited from serving in the army, and thus, as St. Jerome noted, "they lost their manly bearing." In the fourth and fifth centuries, they were directed by the laws of the Christian-Roman Empire into the most degrading occupations and reduced practically to slavery, in order to destroy among them any hope of regaining their social and political freedom. (Hay's *Europe and The Jews*, p.23)

As a result largely of ecclesiastical bigotry, the word 'Jew', during the second half of the fifth century, was often a term of opprobrium. Further, almost every misfortune the Jews suffered was commonly regarded by Christians as evidence of Divine punishment. Thus Eusebius (260?–340?) declared in his *Church History* his intention "to recount the misfortunes which immediately came upon the whole Jewish nation in consequence of their plots against our Saviour" (Book I, chapter i). Sulpicius Severus (360?–410?), Latin Christian writer, asserted: "The Jews are thus punished and exiled throughout the whole world, for no other account than for the impious hands they laid upon Christ" (*Historia Sacra*, Book II, chap. XXX). Severus was writing of the fall of Jerusalem (A.D. 70), in which perhaps as many as a million people were killed. Indeed, as was noted in Chapter 7, Jesus' curse of the fig tree (Mark 11:12–14) has often been treated as symbolizing the destruction of Jerusalem as punishment of Jews for disbelief. Like many other pious Christians, Severus saw in the Jerusalem massacre a Divine signature, much as many people today view the disease AIDS as punishment of homosexuals.

The most popular view of the Middle Ages was that 'the Jews' were guilty of deicide, that they had acted with deliberate malice, and that the entire Jewish people were forever guilty. The view was not universal, but it was overwhelmingly predominant, supported by most of the church's best and most influential minds. It is easy to understand how Christians who treated some Biblical verses with absolute certitude could have come to think like Severus. For if God would send homicidal bears to punish wise-cracking children (2 Kings 2:23–24), it may have seemed difficult to see why He would restrain His wrath when dealing with Enemies of the Light. It is also easy to understand how Christians produced Jewish ghettoes and oppressive anti-Jewish laws; the psychological distance between believing that Jews deserve Divine punishment and wanting to contribute to their suffering is not far. Thus, Christians arrived at the first step (believing that Jews were evil and condemned) by accepting superficial interpretations of certain Biblical verses.

Although the first two hundred years of Christian-Roman rule were oppressive for Jews, the medieval period (A.D. 500–1500) was one of the saddest periods for the Jewish people. Such an evaluation is hardly novel; many Christian theologians concur. Biblical scholar, Frank Eakin, Jr., writes:

> . . . [the medieval period] is one of the most sordid eras in church history, for unfortunately the responsibility, and thus guilt, for this extensive persecution and death falls upon the church. (Frank E. Eakin, Jr., *Religion in Western Culture: Selected Issues* [Washington, D.C.: University Press of America, 1977], p.153)

William L. Reese summarizes some of the highlights of Christian oppression:

> From the time of Justinian in the 6th century A.D., legislation against heretics was applied to the Jews. In 535 the Synod of Clermont decreed that Jews were not to be allowed to hold public office. The Third Synod of Orleans in 538 decreed that Jews were not to be allowed on the streets during Passion Week. The ravaging of ghettoes during the crusades forced an eastward migration of European Jews to Poland and Russia. The Fourth Lateran Council of 1215 called for special dress for Jews, a distinctive badge and, once again, their expulsion from public office. In 1269 the Synod of Breslau called for compulsory ghettoes. The Council of Basel in 1434 denied academic degrees to Jews. The Inquisition specifically singled out the conversion of Jews as one of its aims, and utilized its inimitable style of evangelism to that

end. Regarded as an internal fifth column, Jews were frequently punished following Islamic victories in the Christian-Muslim struggles. In 1492 the Jews were forcibly expelled from Spain, the family of Spinoza among them. In 1497 came expulsion from Portugal. (William L. Reese, 'Christianity and the Final Solution', *The Philosophical Forum*, Vol. XVI, Nos. 1–2, Fall–Winter 1984–1985, p.142)

THE LEGACY OF 'CHRISTIAN' ANTI-JEWISH HATRED

After 1500 the only two European countries in which Jews were allowed to survive as a continuous community were Germany and Italy. But even there Jews were hardly welcome; they were often restricted to subservient positions that Christians tended to dislike, such as money-lending. After Luther nailed his ninety-five theses to the door of the castle church in Wittenberg on October 31, 1517, he expected Jews to join him in attacking the Catholic Church. When they did not join him, Luther expressed a hatred of Jews that inspired the most hateful Nazis. He wrote:

> What then shall we Christians do with this depraved and damned people of the Jews? . . . I will give my faithful advice: First, that one should set fire to their synagogues. . . . Then that one should also break down and destroy their houses. . . . That one should drive them out of the country. (*Sämtliche Schriften* ['Collected Writings'], XX)

Luther's religious and theological intolerance well reflected the intolerance found in his favorite Gospel, that of John; and his desire to see burning synagogues simply followed a precedent set by St. Ambrose. Just as Luther was influenced by at least 1400 years of religious bigotry, so the Nazis could draw on Luther, in honor of whose birthday the Nazis committed their first large-scale pogrom (attack on a Jewish ghetto) in November 1938. "Verily a hopeless, wicked, venomous and devilish thing," Luther wrote, "is the existence of these Jews, who for fourteen hundred years have been, and still are, our pest, torment, and misfortune. They are just devils and nothing more" (Hartmann Grisar, *Luther*, IV, 286). Luther said that "all the blood kindred of Christ" will rightly burn in Hell, for "they are rightly served, even according to their own words they spoke to Pilate." Matthew 27:25 must have found a special place in Luther's hateful heart. It is not surprising that Julius Streicher, in his defense at Nuremberg, argued that he simply put into effect Luther's doctrine about Jews. Streicher was exaggerating, but not by much. It is also not surprising that, when Hitler was asked in 1933 what he planned to do about the Jews, he responded that he would do to them what Christians had been preaching for 2000 years (F.M. Schweitzer, *A History of the Jews Since the First Century A.D.* [New York: Macmillan, 1971], p. 222, cited in Eckardt's *Your People, My People*, pp. 24–25). Hitler knew quite well that Christians have called Jews Christ-killers and children of Satan for nearly 2,000 years. It is indeed unfortunate for Hitler to have taken to heart the notions of those Christians who tragically believed that Jews were "devils."

CONCLUSION

Some verses in the Bible are not easy to understand. Sometimes they have been read and applied without a complete awareness of their meanings, origins, and implications; but the consequences of such uncritical acceptance of Biblical verses are written clearly in history, often in blood.

Many readers of the Bible, unfortunately, do not realize that some verses, including those that can promote intolerance of other people and other beliefs, may not be quite what they seem. Understanding the historical conditions that most likely influenced Biblical authors helps dramatically to explain the sources of much confusion. That subject will be discussed in Chapter 11.

Yet readers of the Bible are not the only people to have had difficulty fully understanding certain verses. Indeed, as will be shown in the next chapter, even some of the New Testament writers themselves, perhaps out of great faith, misunderstood some Old Testament verses.

CHAPTER 10

Problematic Interpretations by New

Testament Authors

Because of their powerful faith in Jesus, New Testament writers interpreted certain Old Testament verses as having been fulfilled in the person of Jesus. They maintained that each of those verses represented Messianic prophecy, and that Jesus therefore must have fulfilled most if not all of them. Thus, they believed that Jesus had to meet certain prerequisites to be the Messiah prophesied in the Old Testament. They interpreted Jesus, therefore, as possessing such Messianic characteristics as, for example, being descended from David, being a 'son of God', being of Virgin Birth, being a 'Nazarene', being one who had triumphantly entered Jerusalem on a donkey, being one who had come out of Egypt, and being born in Bethlehem. Yet a number of those interpretations appear to have misconstrued the original context of the Old Testament or simply inaccurately described Jesus.

Many non-fundamentalist Christians do not feel impelled to believe that Jesus must have fulfilled *all* the Messianic prophecies cited in the New Testament. Most fundamentalists, however, because of their belief in Biblical inerrancy, feel impelled to believe that no New Testament writer could ever have, even unintentionally, mistranslated, misinterpreted, misunderstood, or otherwise misused any Old Testament verses. Those fundamentalists must regard as entirely accurate *every* New Testament statement that describes Jesus as having fulfilled certain prophecies.

Before discussing some of those problematic New Testament interpretations, it is well briefly to consider some of the ideas associated with the Hebrew Messiah. The aim here is not to establish or refute the claim that Jesus was the Messiah, but only to point out that the Old Testament contains many *different* conceptions of what a Messiah was. Indeed, if Jesus was not the Messiah in one sense, he could still be the Messiah in another sense.

In early Hebrew thought, the term 'Messiah' could be used to describe prophets, priests, or kings, and conveyed the idea of a literal anointment (for example, 1 Samuel 10:1). The term came eventually to be used to refer to any person who was fulfilling a Divine mission, including non-Israelites. Accordingly, Cyrus, the king of Persia, was called "God's anointed" (Isaiah 45:1).

The term came to describe many different conceptions of Divinely appointed people. At one period of Biblical history, the Messiah was considered an ideal king who would be the perfect judge; at another period he was viewed as a great conqueror whose dominion would be universal; and at still another period he was a leader whose reign would signal the beginning of a new world of peace and spiritual knowledge.

According to one conception, the Messiah was conceived as the New Moses (Deuteronomy 18:18), who would interpret the Pentateuch ('Five Books of Moses') with original insight and enable the people to enjoy their relationship with God. To some degree Matthew saw Jesus as fulfilling that role (Matthew 5:21–28).

On another conception, the Messiah was conceived as an earthly king of Davidic descent who would fulfill God's promise of Davidic rule over the Hebrew people (2 Samuel 7:10–16). To a degree Matthew and Luke perceived Jesus as restoring Davidic rule. Although they did not appear to treat Jesus as an earthly king, they did picture him as being related to David and as having been born in Bethlehem, the "City of David."

The Messiah was also at times viewed as a suffering servant (as in Isaiah 42:1; 49:1–6; 50:4–11; and 52:13–53:12), and that conception has been interpreted by many people as referring to the nation of Israel itself, which, though persecuted, would serve as a "light to the nations" (Isaiah 42:6;

49:6). Some of the New Testament writers viewed Jesus as the suffering-servant Messiah.

Those are just a few of the principal ideas associated with Messianic conceptions. (For further examples, see such works as Joseph Klausner's *The Messianic Idea in Israel* and Helmer Ringgren's *The Messiah in the Old Testament.*) The point of this chapter is not to affirm or deny Jesus' Messiahship, but to indicate problems with some of the New Testament interpretations of Old Testament Messianic prophecies. For one of the dangers risked by fundamentalists who believe in the doctrine of inerrancy is that they may be unable to detect such problems.

THE MESSIAH AS A DESCENDANT OF DAVID

Because certain verses in the Old Testament (for example, Amos 9:11–12; Isaiah 9:6–7) describe the Messiah as a descendant of David, Matthew and Luke may have been inclined to perceive Jesus as having been descended from David. But is the Davidic claim necessarily plausible? Note that the Biblical Jesus virtually denied that he was of Davidic descent when he questioned how David could have referred to his son as "Lord". The Biblical Jesus said:

> Why do you religious teachers claim that the Messiah must be a descendant of King David? For David himself said . . . "God said to my Lord, sit at my right hand until I make your enemies your footstool." Since David called him his Lord, how can he be his *son*?" (Mark 12:35–37; and similarly, Matthew 22:41–46; Luke 20:41–44)

In other words, the Biblical Jesus argued that if the Messiah were David's son, David would definitely not have called the Messiah "Lord". What is more, the genealogies of Jesus (in Matthew 1:1–17 and Luke 3:23–28) seek to prove Jesus' Davidic ancestry, yet they show only paternal Davidic descent, and that has no validity since he was presumably of Virgin Birth. Moreover, where Matthew's list can be checked against similar lists in the Old Testament (as in the first chapters of 1 Chronicles), it contains discrepancies. (Additional deficiencies in the genealogies are discussed in the next chapter.)

The Messiah as a 'Son of God' in the Old Testament Sense

When Peter referred to Jesus as the Son of the living God (Matthew 16:16), the Son of God idea was clearly rooted in verses like 2 Samuel 7:14, 16 and Psalm 2:7–9, in which simply the king of Israel is regarded as a son of God.

> [God said to David:] For when you die, I will put one of your sons upon your throne and I will make his kingdom strong. . . . I will be his father and he shall be my son. If he sins, I will use other nations to punish him. . . . Your family shall rule my kingdom forever. (2 Samuel 7:14, 16)

> [David, the King of Israel and the traditionally ascribed author of this Psalm, said:] I will reveal the everlasting purposes of God, for the Lord has said to me, "You are my Son. This is your Coronation Day. Today I am giving you your glory." Only ask, and I will give you all the nations of the world. Rule them with an iron rod; smash them like clay pots! (Psalm 2:7–9)

It must be kept in mind that most kings in the Biblical era, whether Hebrew or Gentile, served as the priestly, as well as executive-military, head of state. Because the Old Testament expression 'son of God' refers to an earthly king, it does not accurately describe Jesus. Further, the expression was never used by Jesus in the Bible to refer to himself or anyone else.

The Virgin Birth as Fulfillment of Old Testament Prophecy

The idea of the Virgin Birth (Matthew 1:23) was clearly rooted in Isaiah 7:14: ". . . the Lord himself will choose the sign—a child shall be born to a virgin! And she shall call him Immanuel." But was the Virgin Birth of Jesus a requirement of the Hebrew Messiah? Consider that Matthew appears to have accepted what is a Greek mistranslation of the Hebrew word for "young woman" in Isaiah 7:14. In fact, *The Living Bible* (on which *The Book* is directly based) explains in its footnote to the Isaiah verse:

> The controversial Hebrew word used here sometimes means "virgin" and sometimes "young woman." Its immediate use here refers to Isaiah's young wife and her newborn son (Isaiah 8:1–4). This, of

course, was not a virgin birth. God's sign was that before this child was old enough to talk (verse 4) the two invading kings would be destroyed.

In fact, Isaiah did not use the Hebrew word that refers unambiguously to virgins, and the context makes clear the implausibility of interpreting the word Isaiah did use to mean 'virgin'. The only reason *The Living Bible* gives for using the word 'virgin' in its paraphrase of Isaiah is that since Matthew interpreted it that way, it must be so.

Much of the book of Isaiah, where the birth of a child is discussed, has been taken as Messianic prophecy. Yet a careful reading of it does not suggest that it should be so viewed. As *The Living Bible* points out, "God's sign was that before this child was old enough to talk . . . the two invading kings would be destroyed." That observation is essentially in agreement with the most plausible interpretation of the verse, that the child described in the seventh chapter of Isaiah is to be a sign to Ahaz, the king of Judah, that he will not be defeated in battle by Pekah, the king of Israel, and Resin, the king of Syria. Most of the surrounding verses, too, are directly related to this child of Isaiah's day, and not most likely to the birth of a Messiah of all mankind born about 750 years later. (There are a number of other reasons for doubting that Isaiah 7:14 referred to a Virgin Birth. We will discuss this further in the next chapter.)

Further, the idea of virgin birth is quite alien to the Old Testament. There are miraculous births in the Old Testament, but they typically involve births of sons either to women well past the age of child-bearing (as in Sarah, Abraham's wife) or someone who has given up hope of ever bearing a child (as in the mothers of Samson and of the prophet Samuel). In the miraculous Old Testament births Yahweh participated, but only to cure women of infertility so that they could bear children in the normal way.

Thus, it seems that Matthew must have misconstrued Isaiah 7:14 when he interpreted it as containing prophecy that the Messiah would be of Virgin Birth; and Jesus' Virgin Birth, therefore, does not relate to Messianic prophecy.

Jesus' Triumphant Entry into Jerusalem as Fulfillment of Old Testament Prophecy

The event of Jesus' triumphant entry into Jerusalem riding along "on a young donkey" (John 12:12–15, and similarly Matthew 21:1–7; Mark 11:1–10; Luke 19:28–35) is claimed to represent Jesus' fulfillment of an Old Testament Messianic prophecy in Zechariah 9:9: "Rejoice greatly, O my people! Shout with joy! For look—your King is coming! He is the Righteous one, the Victor! Yet he is lowly, riding on a donkey's ass." Yet Zechariah was most likely not alluding to Jesus, since the preceding verses clearly refer to earthly lands of Zechariah's time (centuries before Jesus' time) that would be conquered by God's anointed earthly king, with no reference to any spiritual kingdom:

> This is the message concerning God's curse on the lands of Hadrach and Damascus. . . . "Doomed is Hamath, near Damascus, and Tyre, and Zidon, too. . . . Though Tyre has armed herself to the hilt, . . . the Lord will dispossess her, and hurl her fortifications into the sea; and she shall be set on fire and burned to the ground.
> "Gaza will huddle in desperation and Ekron will shake with terror, for their hopes that Tyre would stop the enemies' advance will all be dashed. Gaza will be conquered, her king killed, and Ashkelon will be completely destroyed.
> "Foreigners will take over the city of Ashdod, the rich city of the Philistines. . . . And I will surround my Temple like a guard to keep invading armies from entering Israel." (Zechariah 9:1–8)

Note further that after the Zechariah 9:9 verse, there is further reference to the destruction of Israel's physical enemies:

> Judah, you are my bow! Ephraim, you are my arrow! Both of you will be my sword of a mighty soldier. . . .
> The Lord shall lead his people as they fight! His arrows shall fly like lightening; the Lord God shall sound the trumpet call and go out against his enemies like a whirlwind off the desert from the south. (Zechariah 9:13–15)

Still further, Matthew (21:7) may have misread Zechariah 9:9. For Matthew had Jesus entering Jerusalem on two animals, not—as in the other Gospels—just one. It is difficult to understand Matthew's description of two animals unless he misunderstood the sense of Zechariah 9:9, which, because of poetic parallelism, can appear to refer to two animals. The discrepancy may reveal an effort by Matthew to bring the verse into closer harmony with the Old Testament verse that he believed to be fulfilled by Jesus' entry into Jerusalem.

Poetic parallelism is a distinctive feature of Hebrew poetry in which the basic idea in one line of poetry is restated in a second, and sometimes third, line. The repeated lines often add clarity to the meaning of the first line. Thus, Mark, for example, could see that the last line of Zechariah 9:9, "and upon a colt the foal of an ass", was simply a poetic repetition of the preceding line, "lowly, and riding upon an ass." Matthew, however, apparently either did not appreciate or did not detect the poetic parallelism. (In addition to Zechariah 9:9, many other examples of poetic parallelism can be found in the Old Testament, including Numbers 23:24; 24:9; Psalm 2:4; and so forth.)

Jesus' Exit from Egypt as Fulfillment of Old Testament Prophecy

The event of Jesus' exit from Egypt (Matthew 2:15) is said to have been in fulfillment of Hosea 11:1, in which reference is made to a "child," God's "son," coming out of Egypt. Matthew 2:14–15, in which Joseph and Jesus are represented as going to Egypt and staying there until Herod died, seem surely to be a misapplication of Hosea 11:1, which says, "When Israel was a child I loved him as a son and brought him out of Egypt." That verse and the verses following it make plain that "son" refers to Israel during its exodus from Egypt, and that "child" refers to Israel's being a young nation at the time. Israel is similarly described as God's "son" in Exodus 4:22 and elsewhere in the Old Testament. The writer of Matthew's Gospel, though, treated Hosea 11:1, which refers to a past event, as a prediction about Jesus. Some fundamentalists, intent upon reconciling Matthew's verse with their presumption of Biblical inerrancy, have maintained that the Hosea verse has a double meaning, referring to both the past and the future. While they are perfectly free to view it in that way, they are ignoring the implausibility (and perhaps even the arbitrariness) of such a contention, and considerably weakening their case for claiming that almost all the events in the Biblical Jesus' life were *clearly* prophesied.

The Messiah as being Born in Bethlehem

Jesus' Bethlehem birth has long been presumed to fulfill Micah 5:2: "O Bethlehem Ephrathah, you are but a small Judean village, yet you will be the birthplace of my King who is alive from everlasting ages past! God will abandon his people to their enemies until the time of Israel's spiritual rebirth; then at last the exile remnants of Israel will rejoin their brethren in their own land." While it is virtually impossible to prove where Jesus was born, there is strong historical evidence that, at the least, Luke's account of Jesus' birth is not *entirely* accurate. According to Luke 2:1–4, Joseph and Mary went from Nazareth to Bethlehem because of a census:

> About this time Caesar Augustus, the Roman Emperor, decreed that a census should be taken throughout the nation. (This census was taken when Quirinius was governor of Syria.) Everyone was required to return to his ancestral home for this registration. And because Joseph was a member of the royal line, he had to go to Bethlehem in Judea, King David's ancient home—journeying there from the Galilean village of Nazareth.

Many historians, however, have long puzzled over why the Roman government would have required a resident of Nazareth—Nazareth not even being under Roman rule at that time but rather under the rule of King Herod's son—to trek to Bethlehem to participate in a census designed to record the number of people there for purposes of taxation. In other words, they have wondered what sense there would have been in taking a census of everyone who had only *ancestral* ties to the region. Such an action would seem as implausible as, for example, a contemporary Israeli citizen going back to Egypt for a census simply because his ancestors had resided there centuries ago.

The claim that Joseph returned to Bethlehem becomes even more puzzling when it is considered that Mark and John give no indication whatsoever of believing that Jesus was born in Bethlehem. Further, there is no historical evidence that a census was taken right before Jesus' birth. Most non-fundamentalists, therefore, can easily acknowledge that, whether or not Jesus was born in Bethlehem, Luke, at least, may have been overzealous in making sure that his account of Jesus' birth meshed with some of the Old Testament Messianic prophecies. Perhaps because of his zeal, Luke committed some historical errors. (More detailed exploration of the census as well as other aspects of the Biblical account of Jesus' birth is contained in the next chapter.)

JESUS' RESIDENCE IN NAZARETH AS FULFILLMENT OF OLD TESTAMENT PROPHECY

Finally, Jesus' Nazareth residence is stated in Matthew 2:23 to be in fulfillment of Old Testament prophecy. Matthew wrote that Joseph made his home in a town called Nazareth, and that this "fulfilled the prediction of the prophets concerning the Messiah, 'He shall be called a Nazarene'." Exactly what quotation Matthew had in mind is uncertain, but what is certain is that the Old Testament never refers to any messiah as a Nazarene in the sense of being an inhabitant of Nazareth. Perhaps Matthew confused 'Nazarene' with 'Nazirite'. In Judges 13:5, Samson's mother is warned by an angel of a forthcoming son who is to fulfill God's purpose: "Your son's hair must never be cut, for he shall be a Nazirite, a special servant of God." Or perhaps Matthew was reflecting the tradition of calling the Messiah the 'Branch' (Hebrew 'netzer'), the new growth from the Davidic line. For example, Zechariah 6:12 refers to the Messiah as "The Branch", and similarly, in Jeremiah 23:5, reference is made to a "righteous Branch". If Matthew was matching 'Nazarene' with 'Nazirite' or 'Netzer', he was not in this case properly interpreting the Old Testament use of those words.

CONCLUSION

Biblical authors, then, were fallible human beings who sometimes viewed Scripture according to their preconceived religious expectations. As human beings, they were influenced by the historical events and cultural beliefs of their day. Indeed, as will be shown in the next chapter, we can appreciate the origin of Biblical inconsistencies and implausibilities by understanding the historical conditions in which the Bible was written.

CHAPTER 11

THE INFLUENCE OF HISTORY UPON

BIBLICAL AUTHORS

Perhaps the most effective way to avoid many of the hazards associated with Christian fundamentalism is to regard a Biblical implausibility or inconsistency, not as a 'perfection' *or even as an 'imperfection'*, but rather as a *reflection* of the beliefs and purposes of its particular author. The aim of this chapter is to consider the historical conditions that may have influenced Biblical writers and produced, therefore, any unreasonable biases, evidently false statements, and inconsistencies.

A GENERAL EXPLANATION

As has been illustrated in earlier chapters, some verses in the Bible can easily be interpreted as portraying God committing atrocities, demanding worship on threat of force, or performing contranatural feats. Sometimes when accepted as part of a true portrait of one's God, many of those depictions of the Biblical God can inspire and 'justify' hatred.

Yet if those negative depictions of God are perceived as stemming from the motives and personalities of the Biblical writers, they can more easily be appreciated, and the wisest use of them can be made. Consider that the Biblical writers were searching for an understanding of God on which they could rely in a world in which floods can cover the land, famines can take away the very sustenance of life, earthquakes can crumble the ground on which one stands, and wars can lay waste to humanity. In a world in which life hangs in the balance and the 'whys' of suffering, hatred, and natural disaster are a mystery, it is natural to seek extra help, and belief in a simplistic conception of God often relieves much anxiety. The Biblical writers, however, were not trying to invent a story-book view of God; they were responding to their times, their fears, and their interests.

The world of the Old Testament writers was a credulous world in which the worshipping of numerous Gods was common. Warring was almost a way of life, and losers often explained their defeats by talk of Divine displeasure. Victories, too, were ascribed to Gods. Prophets were said to perform bizarre and seemingly contranatural feats to 'prove' that they possessed the Divine sanction of their particular Gods. The prophets assisted men who asked their Gods for help in conquering warring neighbors. Many people feared worshipping the Gods of other tribes and nations, lest they should have offended their Gods. The leaders were both temporal and spiritual, believed to be Divinely anointed as kings.

The Gods typically shared human frailties: They could be jealous (like the depiction of the Biblical God in Exodus 20:5), warlike (Exodus 15:3), deceptive (Exodus 7:3–4), egocentric (Exodus 9:15–16; 2 Samuel 7:23), and ethnocentric (Leviticus 20:23). Such ethnocentrism reflected a nation's desire to promote its Gods over the influence of foreign nations and their Gods, and most of the other characteristics were needed to try to justify the conquering of other nations.

RELIGIOUS BELIEFS IN THE OLD TESTAMENT

The 'Yahwehist' conception of God was introduced to the Hebrews by Moses (Exodus 3:15, 6:3), and the Hebrews carried Yahweh in a box (ark of the covenant) into battle, believing that His presence gave them their victories (Numbers 10:35–36). The zeal for Yahweh was fostered both by their belief that He had helped them conquer the land and by their ongoing struggle against foreign nations and the Gods of those nations.

A variety of religious faiths developed in the history of Israel. As a consequence of their interaction with Canaanite neighbors and spouses, the Hebrews worshipped Canaanite deities before the Exodus, and some Hebrews worshipped them even after the Exodus. That the Hebrews at times viewed God as consisting of more than one entity (polytheism) is evident from the Old Testament, where, for example,

Yahweh is described as greater than all other Gods (Exodus 18:11), and is exalted far above all other Gods (Psalm 97:9). The Hebrews came increasingly to identify the Canaanite God 'El' with Yahweh, so that they were no longer regarded as two Gods but as one God with two different names. Consequently, in Hebrew texts the two names occur in parallel in Balaam's poem (Numbers 23:8), and 'El Yahweh' occurs in Psalm 85:8. Combining deities was fairly common in many ancient religions.

The monotheism of Israel did not develop overnight but developed gradually. For example, in the eighth century B.C., the prophets Amos and Isaiah believed that, while Yahweh might not be the only God, He was the only God to control the destinies of everyone and not just the Hebrews (Amos 9:7; Isaiah 10:5–6). Genuine monotheism does, though, appear in the Deuteronomic Code (Deuteronomy 4:35) and in Isaiah (Isaiah 43:10–11).

Throughout the Old Testament period the Hebrews often struggled between the worship of Yahweh and the worship of foreign Gods. The Old Testament bears witness to that struggle, as when it documents the occasions on which the Hebrew kings opposed the pagan religions. Very much concerned to retain their religious and cultural identity, Hebrew kings would from time to time forbid the adoption of pagan rituals. Thus, late in the tenth century Asa, king of Judah, removed Canaanite idols (1 Kings 15:12–14), and in the ninth century Jehu, king of Israel, executed all the Baal worshippers (2 Kings 10:15–28). Similarly, Hezekiah, king of Judah in the eighth century, removed Canaanite sanctuaries and idols (2 Kings 18:4); the Judean King Josiah, during the seventh century, removed the Baalism and astralism introduced by Manasseh and restored the worship of Yahweh in the temple (2 Kings 21:3–9).

During exile some Hebrews in Babylon were so afraid of losing their religious and cultural identity that they became particularly strict about observing the Sabbath and practicing circumcision. That fear was evident in Ezra, who, on returning to his homeland, required Hebrews there to divorce their Gentile wives as well as to observe the Sabbath and support the temple (Ezra 9:1–10:44; similar occurrences are described in Nehemiah 13:23–25 and elsewhere). The Hasmoneans in the second century reflected a similar concern for cultural identity when they fought against the influence of Greek religion and displayed hostility to the rival but similar religion of the Samaritans, whose temple on Mount Gerizim was destroyed by the Hasmonean ruler John Hyrcanus.

The covenants made between the Hebrews and Yahweh were prevalent in Near Eastern religions and reflected the custom of ascribing to Gods the concepts and practices applied to kings. For example, since the institution of slavery was part of the social structure in all countries of the ancient Near East, it is not surprising that the Old Testament should contain laws governing slavery (Exodus 21; Leviticus 25; Deuteronomy 15).

That the Hebrews used and developed some of the laws of their neighbors is demonstrable. It is well known, for example, that the Mosaic code to some degree reflects the laws of Hammurabi, king of Babylonia in the eighteenth century B.C. Like Hammurabi's legal code, the Mosaic code included the law of retaliation ("an eye for an eye"; Exodus 21:24) and punished theft by death. In some respects, Hammurabi's code was more liberal and humane (as in its allowing women and not just men to divorce their spouses), and in some respects it was less humane and just (as in its treating aristocrats and commoners differently).

Variations in Writing Practices and Styles of Old Testament Authors

Although the Hebrews were enormously concerned with their history, they were not always primarily concerned to record it with meticulous accuracy. For example, when the author of a book in the Hebrew Scriptures was unknown, the Hebrews would sometimes attribute the book to a hero in the past to give the book authority. Accordingly, the original five books of the Bible were ascribed to Moses, many of the Psalms to David, and many of the Proverbs to Solomon. (See Chapter 8 for examples of internal evidence illustrating that those and other Biblical books were most likely not written by their supposed authors.) Sometimes, Biblical authors would rewrite stories, reflecting their current ideas and values. There are differences, for example, between the histories given in 1 and 2 Chronicles on the one hand and 2 Samuel and 1 and 2 Kings on the other. Both parts of the Bible purport to narrate Hebraic history from the reign of David to the exile of Jews in Babylon (from about 1000 to 587 B.C.). Note that the Chronicler retold the story, and that he constructed genealogies that gave more prestige to the lower order of priests (the Levites). Note further that he sometimes ascribed to David's period conditions that existed not then but in the Chronicler's time, as when he divided the Levites into four groups: overseers, officers and judges, gatekeepers, and singers (1 Chronicles 23:2–5). Note finally that there is reason to believe that he exaggerated the size of the armies in ancient times, as when he maintained that Asa, the king of Judah, had an army of 580,000 men who, with Yahweh's support, killed the entire army of one million Ethiopians (2 Chronicles 14:8–13). In fact, such a battle is not even mentioned in the earlier account of Asa's reign (1 Kings 15–16).

Sometimes Biblical writers retold stories in such a way as to have made them conform to current theological beliefs. For example, there are two Biblical versions of King David's ill-starred census. In the older version (2 Samuel 24:1) it is the Lord who inspired David to take the census; in the later version (1 Chronicles 21:1) it is Satan. The discrepancy is easily explained: The Jewish belief in Satan was not firmly established during the writing of the older version, at which time it was Yahweh who brought both weal *and* woe.

In short, internal Biblical evidence demonstrates that Biblical writers would on occasion rewrite stories, sometimes even contradicting earlier versions. Sometimes differences in vocabulary are indications that at least two authors were writing a particular book. Such differences are particularly profound when different sections of a book use different terms for the same thing. Consider, for example, the two different creation stories. While one account consistently uses the Hebrew word for 'God', the other consistently uses the Hebrew expression for 'Lord God'. Further, in one of the accounts the Hebrew word for 'create' occurs frequently, whereas in the other account it never appears. The two versions of creation contain not only substantial linguistic differences but also self-contradictions, at least when regarded as one narrative. For example, Creation took only one day in one account, but took six days in the other.

Sometimes differences in writing style are so pronounced that it should be obvious that the styles belong to different writers. For example, Isaiah's style in his own composition (in Isaiah 1–39) is substantially different from the style of Isaiah 40–55. Whereas the first style contains remarkably concise and concrete poetry, the latter style is often verbose, repetitious, and vague. To see how one style can be inserted into another, consider 'Hannah's Prayer' in 1 Samuel 2:1–10. The style is inappropriate for its context, in which one would expect an impromptu prayer rather than a formal hymn. Further, the content of the prayer is also inappropriate, since it does not refer to Hannah's situation, but rather is a hymn for group singing. Still further, although the prayer is set in a context in which Hannah is pledging her son Samuel to the Lord, the prayer or hymn itself concerns not Samuel but a king.

Sometimes the tone of a book changes so abruptly that it is obvious that editors have inserted their own thoughts. Consider, for example, the book of Amos, in which the predominant outlook reflects Amos's gloominess and indignation at unrighteousness. There is evidence suggesting that another writer tried to change the tone of the book by some insertions, such as the last five verses. The additions, unlike Amos's outlook generally, display optimism, in which God does not predict despair but hope: All the hills shall flow with sweet wine and Israel will have good fortune. Those additions help to illustrate that an editor tried to change the tone of Amos from despair to hope.

DIFFERENCES AMONG NEW TESTAMENT WRITERS

There is strong evidence that the writers of the Gospels of Matthew and Luke copied large portions of Mark's Gospel and made additions, subtractions, and refinements. For several reasons most Biblical scholars believe that Mark's Gospel is the oldest Gospel, and that it was a source for the writers of Matthew and Luke.

First, Mark's Gospel is, stylistically speaking, the crudest Gospel in the Greek. Rarely will the grammar and diction of a derivative work be far inferior to the original document. If the writer of Mark had copied from Matthew and Luke, his literary style often would have been at least almost as sophisticated as the style of those Gospels. Second, almost all Mark's stories and sayings are also in Matthew and Luke and usually in the same order. Normally, when one of them reproduced Mark's material in a different order, the other will retain the material in Mark's order. Third, although both Matthew and Luke tend to follow Mark's narrative closely, whenever one or both differ from Mark, they will rarely agree with each other. Fourth, and finally, the differences between Matthew and Luke on the one hand and Mark on the other are usually due to differences in points of view. On the basis of the evidence it is reasonable to believe that Matthew and Luke both used Mark as a source and adapted the material to their beliefs and purposes. Certainly, this copying and adapting would help to explain why some stories and teachings among those Gospels appear contradictory.

From the time of the writing of the Gospel of Mark to that of the writing of the Gospels of Matthew and Luke, the personality of Jesus evidently is progressively magnified in some respects: In Mark he has obviously human characteristics and even foibles. There he wonders, asks questions, and even yields to emotion, as when he becomes angry with the Pharisees who objected to his healing a man with a paralyzed hand on the Sabbath (Mark 3:1–6). In Matthew and Luke, Jesus is not described as such. There, for example, he is not represented as angered by the Pharisees' objection to that healing.

In Mark, Jesus reportedly *"couldn't"* do *any* mighty miracles in front of his own countrymen because of their unbelief, and he had difficulty in accepting the fact that they "wouldn't" believe in him (Mark 6:1–6). Yet in Matthew Jesus *did* do at least "a few great miracles" (Matthew 13:58).

It is in the Gospel of John that Jesus is depicted as most godlike. In Mark, Jesus humbly claims that he is not good, that only God is good (Mark 10:17–18), whereas in John, Jesus proclaims himself to be the Light of the world (John 8:12). It is in the Gospel of John where Jesus' disciples never desert him, where he is sure of his mission from the start, where he is, in some sense, a pre-existent son of God (John 8:58), a metaphysical principle. It is there that Jesus' final words from the Cross are "It is finished" (John 19:30) and not "My God, my God, why have you forsaken me?" (Matthew 27:46).

The explanation not only for why John was willing to portray a nearly superhuman Jesus but also for why the other Gospels were *not* willing to, is most easily recognized when viewed within their historical context. The writer of John was writing at a later period, when Christianity contained many Gentile converts and was reaching out for more. Many of those converts had no problems with regarding Jesus as either a superhuman being or even an incarnate God.

The idea of an incarnate God, though, conflicted with the uncompromising monotheism of orthodox Judaism in the time of Jesus. Most Jews were looking not for incarnate Gods but for a this-worldly political Messiah who would restore Jewish political autonomy. Many Jews were hoping for an earthly human leader of a new Jewish kingdom, and that was what, at least to some degree, the writer of Matthew's Gospel provided them. For his accounts of Jesus' life often portray Jesus as fulfilling a number of different strands of Old Testament Messianic prophecy. The author of Matthew's Gospel was Jewish and saw Jesus' mission as confined primarily though perhaps not exclusively to the Jewish people. For that reason it is not surprising that in the stories recorded in Matthew Jesus implies that Gentiles are "dogs" (15:26), instructs his disciples to preach only to Jews (10:5–6), and commands punctilious obedience to every letter of the Mosaic law (5:17–20). None of which is to deny that the writer of Matthew sometimes presented Jesus as helping Gentiles and as welcoming them to the Kingdom of God; the point is rather that, because of the writer's largely Jewish audience and his conception of the Jewish Messiah, he recorded strongly Jewish and sometimes even anti-Gentile sentiments that, for example, the writer of Luke's Gospel (possibly a Gentile) did not record.

Indeed, the writer of Luke not only avoided ascribing to Jesus any extremely sectarian and anti-Gentile utterances (as in Matthew 15:26); he almost seems to have gone out of his way to present Jesus as pro-Gentile, as in the parable of the good Samaritan (Luke 10:29–37), where Jews are, if anything, 'the bad guys'. By the time the Gospel of John was written (perhaps A.D. 90–100) there was widespread antagonism between Christians and unconverted Jews. Jewish-Christian relations had degenerated even since the writing of Matthew's Gospel (A.D. 85–90), when Christians and unconverted Jews were still in dialogue. The tension between Jews and Christians is evident in John's Gospel, where Christians are to be "excommunicated" from the synagogues (9:22; 16:2) and unconverted Jews are described as children of the devil (8:44). (For further discussion on the Fourth Evangelist's opposition to unChristianized Judaism, see Chapter 9.)

The point to seize here is that Biblical writers were neither Divinely operated photocopiers nor writers of fairy tales, but were men interlarding history with a theology reflecting their beliefs and purposes.

THE VIRGIN BIRTH CLAIM

A reason the writers of Matthew and Luke interpreted Jesus as being of Virgin Birth could have been that it was a traditional way of glorifying great people and a useful way, in this case, of replying to anyone who might accuse Jesus of being of illegitimate birth. (Please note that our purpose here is *not* to suggest that Jesus was of illegitimate birth, but only that the Virgin Birth claim may have been advanced to answer any such accusation.)

Claims of virgin birth were a common way of glorifying famous people and mythological heroes of ancient times. For example, Julius Caesar, Augustus, Aristomenes, Alexander the Great, Plato, Cyrus, the elder Scipio, Egyptian Pharaohs, the Buddha, Hermes, Mithra, Attis-Adonis, Hercules,

Cybele, Demeter, Leo, and Vulcan —all were thought of as virgin-born in at least some traditions.

Further, the claim may have particularly appealed to the writers of Matthew and Luke, who perhaps advanced it to respond to any possible accusations that Jesus might be of illegitimate birth. Consider, for example, their apparent reaction to a scene first described in the Gospel of Mark. In Mark, Jesus' fellow citizens of Nazareth refer to Jesus not as Joseph's son but as Mary's son (6:3). When the same scene is repeated in Matthew and Luke—Gospels written later than Mark— Jesus is referred to as either the carpenter's son (Matthew 13:55–56) or Joseph's son (Luke 4:22). The change may have been made to avoid giving readers the impression that Jesus could have been of illegitimate birth. For if those citizens of Nazareth believed that Joseph was Jesus' father, they would almost certainly have referred to Jesus as Joseph's son. The traditional nomenclature referred to a person by his patronymic, as in 'Abel the son of Adam'. A person was referred to as the son of his mother only if the name of the father was unknown. The version of the story in Mark, then, could have left its readers with the impression that Jesus was of illegitimate birth, but Matthew's and Luke's apparent revisions in effect negated that potential impression.

Doubts about Jesus' legitimacy, however, may have already begun to surface during the time of the Gospels, and thus, perhaps, the writers of Matthew and Luke were especially eager to neutralize those negative rumors. The presence of doubt about Jesus' legitimacy is suggested in, for example, the Gospel of John (8:41). During a heated argument "the Jews" taunt Jesus by saying, "We were not born out of wedlock—our true Father is God himself." (Our italics. The emphasis here is on the "we" because that is the force of the Greek; the pronoun 'we' is being used in a context in which it would normally be omitted, the subject being already expressed in the Greek verb ending.)

A pagan tradition that Jesus was illegitimate also existed at that time. Celsus, a pagan who wrote in A.D. 180, claimed that Jesus' father was a Roman soldier (Panathera), and that

Joseph rejected Mary so that she had to give birth to Jesus secretly. (Although the story may be entirely apocryphal, it is one possible explanation for Joseph's surprise at Mary's pregnancy [Matthew 1:18–19] and his virtual disappearance from the narrative after Jesus' birth.)

In any case, if the writers of Matthew and Luke were willing to make alterations to Mark's story out of concern over negative rumors about Jesus' legitimacy, they may have been equally willing to advance the Virgin Birth claim out of similar concern. Further, it is significant that neither Mark's Gospel nor Paul's epistles contain the claim. If Mark and Paul had been aware that Jesus was born of a virgin, they would almost certainly have mentioned it, especially since their non-Jewish readers would have been particularly impressed.

Still further, Matthew's and Luke's story of a Virgin Birth was supposed to represent Jesus' fulfillment of an Old Testament Messianic prophecy. Unfortunately, however high-minded the motivation for the story may have been, it seems to have distorted the meaning of Isaiah 7:14, the prophecy that a child would be born to a young woman ('almah' in Hebrew). As pointed out in the previous chapter, the verse in Isaiah almost certainly does not mean 'virgin' ('bethulah' in Hebrew). Nor can it plausibly be taken to refer to Jesus' birth, and no miraculous births described in the Old Testament were ever fatherless. It is important to understand that the author of Matthew most likely used the Greek translation of the Hebrew Scripture (known as the Septuagint), which was the most popular translation in Jesus' day. While the Hebrew language contains words that distinguish between simply a 'young woman' or 'maiden' (almah) and a 'virgin' (bethulah), the Greek language is not so clear. While there is a word, 'neanis,' in Greek that would mean 'maiden,' it is rare; and probably for that reason the Septuagint translators chose the much more common 'parthenos' (virgin) as a translation of 'almah.' Although no one can know whether the author of Matthew was aware of the dubiousness of the Greek translation of Isaiah 7:14, that translation apparently allowed him to glorify Jesus and to reduce any suspicions of illegitimacy.

'PROOF-TEXTING' AND JEWISH MESSIANIC FULFILLMENT

The claim in Matthew and Luke that Jesus was of Virgin Birth is only one example among many of how the Evangelists cited Old Testament Scripture to help prove that Jesus fulfilled numerous types of Old Testament Messianic prophecy. The following table illustrates a few examples of that 'proof-texting' by Matthew.

Matthew	Jewish Scripture	Incident from the life of Jesus
2:15	Hosea 11:1	The flight to Egypt
2:17–18	Jeremiah 31:15	The massacre of innocents
2:23	Unknown; Isaiah 11:1	Jesus dwells in Nazareth
4:14–16	Isaiah 9:1–2	Jesus moves to Capernaum
8:17	Isaiah 53:4	The healing ministry of Jesus
12:17–21	Isaiah 42:1–4	The healing ministry of Jesus
13:35	Psalm 78:2	Jesus' teaching in parables
21:4–5	Isaiah 62:11; Zechariah 9:9	Jesus' entry into Jerusalem
27:9–10	Zechariah 11:12–13; Jeremiah 18:1–13; 32:6–15	The fate of Jesus

In the previous chapter, internal Biblical evidence was presented suggesting that many of those proof-texts represent distorted or misinterpreted Old Testament verses. Indeed, such proof-texting can lead to implausible historical claims, as when Matthew reports that Herod killed all the male infants of Bethlehem (Matthew 2:16), supposedly fulfilling Jeremiah 31:15.

Did Herod's massacre of the babies actually occur? This is dubious because Herod's reign is well documented, and there is no contemporary record of that spectacular atrocity. If Herod had committed such a slaughter, the Jewish historian Josephus would almost certainly have recorded it. That claim is also Biblically dubious because, like many of Matthew's proof-texts, it distorts the context of Old Testament verses. The Jeremiah 31:15 verse has nothing to do with slaughtering of children. In that verse, "there is bitter weeping—Rachel weeping for her children, . . . for they are gone." Yet the next two verses make clear that the reference is to the exile of Rachel's children (probably the Jewish people) into "the distant land of the enemy", and that, in fact, the children "will come again to their own land."

Proof-texting can lead also to Biblical contradictions, as when Matthew describes Jesus as having two animals (Matthew 21:7) instead of one (Mark 11:7; Luke 19:35) to prove that Jesus' entry into Jerusalem fulfilled Zechariah 9:9; or when Matthew, to help establish Jesus' fulfillment of certain verses in Jeremiah and Zechariah, reports that Judas hanged himself (Matthew 27:3–5) instead of that he fell headlong and burst open (Acts 1:18).

THE ACCOUNTS OF JESUS' BETHLEHEM BIRTH

In Jesus' day, the Jewish idea of the future Messiah included the view that he would be born in Bethlehem, thus fulfilling Micah 5:2, an Old Testament Messianic prophecy. The writers of Matthew and Luke may have believed, therefore, that Jesus had been born in Bethlehem. Or, quite conceivably, they may have believed that Bethlehem birth was *not* a significant prerequisite for the Messiah and, therefore, that Jesus was *not* born in Bethlehem. In any case, many if not most of their readers were Jewish, and most likely held the traditional Jewish view that to be the Messiah one had to be born in Bethlehem. The writers of Matthew and Luke apparently felt, therefore, that they had to present explanations of how Jesus, who was associated with Nazareth, could have been born in Bethlehem.

Matthew's account simply gives the impression that Bethlehem was the permanent home of Joseph and Mary, and that Jesus was born there in a house (2:11). Matthew explains that Joseph feared Herod's son, who had succeeded his father as king of Judea, and implies that for that reason they *later* settled in Nazareth (2:22).

Such an explanation could be plausible if it were not for the following facts:

1. Mark, the oldest Gospel, contains no mention of the Bethlehem birth and gives the impression that Jesus was always from Nazareth.

2. John does not present a claim of Bethlehem birth. The Gospel, in fact, relates an incident that appears to contradict the claim: A crowd of people are divided over the question of Jesus' Messiahship, on the ground that Jesus came from Galilee and was neither born in Bethlehem nor descended from David (John 7:40–43). Further, neither Jesus nor his disciples challenge the crowd's assumption that he does not match the Messianic tradition of being born in Bethlehem and of Davidic descent.

3. Luke presents a highly implausible story to explain why Joseph and Mary supposedly left Nazareth and went to Bethlehem to give birth to Jesus. The story also seems to contradict Matthew's. For had Bethlehem been the normal residence of Joseph and Mary, as Matthew's Gospel claims, it is difficult to see why Luke would have resorted to such a story.

To appreciate the difficulties in Luke's account, one must look at its historical background. Since Jesus lived in a time in which travel was slow and troublesome and in which people normally spent their whole lives within a few miles of their birthplaces, Luke required an explanation for why Jesus, who was associated in his day with Nazareth, happened to have been born far away from home. Luke's explanation refers to a Roman census, requiring everyone to return to his own (native) city (2:3). Since Joseph was supposedly born in Bethlehem, he and Mary ventured to that city.

Although the story is superficially plausible, its plausibility is significantly weakened when viewed with historical sensitivity. First, the story presents the Roman government as conducting a census for taxation for which it required people to be counted not where they were currently living and paying taxes but where they were born. The difficulty there is that if the census was for determining the amount of taxes each citizen would be required to pay in each locality, there was no point whatever in requiring people to go to their birthplaces, needlessly clogging the roads and endangering themselves and others. If Joseph was, as Luke reports, resident in Nazareth, his travelling to his ancestral birthplace for a Roman census is not very plausible. There is no historical evidence that the Romans *ever* required people to go to their birthplaces for the purpose of a census.

Further, Luke's statement (2:1–3) that the census was taken under the Syrian governor Quirinius is historically unlikely. For although Quirinius took a census, he took it about A.D. 6 or 7, according to historical records such as Josephus's *Antiquities of the Jews* (18:1). Josephus noted that Quirinius took a census shortly after Judea had been annexed by Rome, about A.D. 6 or 7. That census could not have been coincident with Jesus' birth if he was born during the lifetime of King Herod (Luke 1:5), who died in 4 *B.C.* In addition, Quirinius would not have taken a *Roman* census about 4 B.C. because Rome had no jurisdiction in either Bethlehem or Nazareth during that time. Since Nazareth was not under Roman rule but had its own ruler (the 'tetrarch' Herod Antipas), it would not have been subject to a Roman census. Thus, to justify the claim that Jesus was born in Bethlehem, Luke's Gospel connects Jesus' birth, which that Gospel dates at 4 B.C., with an event that happened about a decade later.

The rest of Luke's account of the Bethlehem birth contains a tissue of implausibilities. For example, it is unlikely that Mary, who was near the end of her pregnancy (Luke 2:5) and who was engaged but not married to Joseph, accompanied Joseph on a perilous journey of about 60–70 miles.

Hence, while the writers of Matthew and Luke were no doubt sincere in their intentions, their accounts of Jesus' Bethlehem birth suggest that they were not entirely certain about how Jesus was born in Bethlehem. Their stories, therefore, reflect the writers' desire to try to fit Jesus more solidly within part of a traditional Messianic role (as in Micah 5:2) expected by many of their readers.

WAS JESUS DESCENDED FROM DAVID?

The main reason that the Bethlehem birth was considered a prerequisite for the Messiah (Micah 5:2) was that Bethlehem was the 'City of David', and according to one view of the Hebrew Messiah, he was to be a descendant of King David (as in Psalm 132:10–12). Yet if the New Testament accounts of

Jesus' Bethlehem birth (and his virgin birth) are sometimes problematic, the claims that Jesus was a descendant of David must become at least open to question.

Here, again, there is strong evidence that some of the Gospel writers injected their own interpretations about Jesus into their writings to reinforce the point that Jesus was the Jewish Messiah. In fact, when they try to strengthen the claim of Davidic descent, Matthew and Luke give sharply divergent genealogies. While Matthew (1:1–17) states that there were 28 generations separating Jesus from King David, Luke (3:23–28) names 41 consecutive generations for the same period. Thus, for Matthew, apparently the 13 additional ancestors of Jesus did not exist.

Further, among all the names that each Gospel writer lists, only three are alike: Zerubbabel, Zerubbabel's father Shealtiel, and Jesus' father Joseph. Since Zerubbabel, who lived about 500 years before Jesus, was a well-known leader in Jewish history, it is not surprising that both Luke and Matthew would have recorded (perhaps rightly) that Zerubbabel was of Davidic descent. It is, however, inconsistent to give Jesus' descent through Joseph, if Jesus was not the biological son of Joseph.

Finally, and perhaps most significantly, Matthew and Luke try to arrive at Zerubbabel by substantially different genealogies, differing even in the name of Joseph's father, whom Matthew calls "Jacob" and Luke calls "Heli".

CONCLUSION

There is a satisfactory explanation for many of the inconsistencies and implausibilities found in the Bible; it requires acknowledging that the Biblical authors were influenced by the beliefs prevalent in their cultures and the historical setting in which they wrote.

CHAPTER 12

Unlocking the Wisdom of the Bible

The major hazards in Christian fundamentalism, and thus the major causes of the doubts and frustration that many fundamentalists feel, are woven into the fundamentalists' approach to the Bible. People who hold the presumption that all the Bible must be 'perfect' may sacrifice the ability to recognize Biblical implausibilities and inconsistencies, and that is a fundamental hazard. For when they are unable to detect a biased statement, a fantastic story, an unjust act, an implausible feat, or a contradictory law, they place their faith in God in a precarious position.

They may be unable to conceive the idea that even one verse in the Bible could possibly depict a less than completely true statement or a less than completely actual event. As a result, instead of viewing that depiction as shaped by historical influences, they may come to view the depiction as part of their own concept of God and humankind. In some people, then, fundamentalism can lead easily to an insulting portrait of God and the world.

In contrast to a fundamentalist approach, a more questioning approach to the Bible can have several important benefits. It can enable people to understand Biblical verses as embedded in historical context and influenced by the culture and personality of each Biblical writer. Understanding that historical context helps interpreters to understand the origin and intention of Biblical verses. A questioning approach can also enable the interpreter to recognize where historical and scientific errors and cultural prejudice may exist, and it can help protect the interpreter from biased interpretations of the Bible.

This approach can also prevent the worship of the Bible, a practice both scientifically and religiously dubious: scientifically dubious because it will lead almost inevitably to misunderstanding the origin and intention of Biblical verses; religiously dubious because it values as ultimate a vehicle rather than what the vehicle attempts to convey.

Finally, a more questioning approach can help people use their reason as well as their emotion, enabling them to use their full humanity in the religious quest. Thus, approaching the Bible in a spirit of questioning helps to assure that people will be liberated by the Bible rather than enslaved by it.

PROGRESS AMONG FUNDAMENTALIST SCHOLARS

While many fundamentalists perceive little if any value in questioning and analyzing the Bible, and often view it as dictated word for word by God, there are some fundamentalist Biblical scholars who are improving their own methods of research and becoming increasingly flexible in their interpretations of the doctrine of Biblical inerrancy. Some of them, especially among Evangelical fundamentalist scholars, are discovering and using scientific methods adopted by many non-fundamentalist Biblical scholars.

One of the most important methods being used is redaction criticism, in which the editorial processes of the Biblical writers themselves are analyzed using linguistic, historical, literary, and other scientific techniques. Using such methods, those fundamentalist scholars are able not only to gain more knowledge about the Bible, but also to recognize some of its inconsistencies. Some of them are able even to acknowledge that Biblical authors may have used various sources, some that were perhaps not entirely accurate; that some of the authors may have sometimes used different literary techniques—poetry, prose, et cetera—to communicate God's will; that they injected at least some of their own opinions and the pre-scientific understandings of the day into at least parts of their writings; and that they were affected by historical conditions.

Yet while those kinds of conclusions are obviously of

some value, the conclusions of fundamentalist scholars are usually reached with the overriding presumption that the Bible must be inerrant. The doctrine of inerrancy may be a somewhat flexible concept, but it *always* requires believing that God communicates perfectly through the Bible. The most liberal position many fundamentalist scholars hold is that there can be 'minor difficulties' in the Bible, but such difficulties, supposedly, can never originate from the authors themselves, can never misrepresent the life and teachings of Jesus, and can never contradict the message God wishes to convey.

And if a difficulty appears irreconcilable with the doctrine of inerrancy, the irreconcilability supposedly stems entirely from modern researchers' 'natural' human ignorance, which prevents them from correctly understanding God's message. If the difficulty is clearly irreconcilable, then it supposedly does not exist in the 'original' Biblical manuscript, which is supposedly perfect (but which no one has found).*

---

*The theory that only the 'original' Biblical manuscripts (autographs) are inerrant makes many of its adherents no less intent upon 'proving' that today's copies (apographs) of the Bible are, for the most part, inerrant, too. The theory, however, is invoked to provide a kind of safety net for those cases where no 'explanation' can be created to mesh with the presumption of inerrancy (for example, in Leviticus 11:6, where hares are said to chew the cud, or in Matthew 23:35, where Jesus misdescribes Zechariah's father by calling him Barachiah instead of Jehoiada [2 Chronicles 23:20–21]). Some of the difficulties of the theory are embodied in the following points:

(1) Given that present-day manuscripts of the Bible reveal pre-scientific thought, historical and cultural influences, a gradual development of moral codes, a human side of Jesus, and misinterpretations of Old Testament verses in New Testament verses, and given that human beings are liable to error, there is little reason to believe that the 'original' manuscripts were inerrant.

(2) The theory requires one to believe that an omnipotent God would miraculously preserve the original Biblical writers from error, while allowing texts which would be the only texts most people could ever know, to become unreliable.

(3) Neither the Biblical Jesus nor any Biblical writers ever draw a distinction between original manuscripts and copies of the Bible.

(4) Many adherents of this theory presume that today's Bibles are mostly error-free. Yet there is no way to be certain exactly where the present texts agree or disagree with the 'original' texts, which are no longer in existence.

In any case, like most theories of inerrancy, the 'original autograph' theory is insensitive to the diversity of understandings displayed in the Bible, which at times reflects human limitations, and which never explicitly teaches the doctrine of inerrancy. (For an excellent discussion of some of those difficulties by moderate Southern Baptists, see *The Unfettered Word* [Robison B. James, ed., Waco, Texas: Word Books, 1987].)

(An excellent example of fundamentalist scholars' treatment of redaction criticism is contained in 'Redaction Criticism: Is It Worth The Risk?' *Christianity Today,* October 18, 1985, pp. 1–12 [Institute Section].)

THE VALUE OF FUNDAMENTALIST RESEARCH

By attempting to 'explain' apparent Biblical inconsistencies and implausibilities within the context of Biblical inerrancy, many fundamentalist scholars' research is of only limited value, but of value nonetheless. For at least it exposes its fundamentalist readers to some Biblical difficulties and thus might provide those readers with the rare opportunity to judge for themselves whether the doctrine of Biblical inerrancy is an adequate approach to the Bible.

For example, fundamentalist scholars sometimes attempt to reconcile modern scientific speculation about the age of the earth, billions of years old, with the Biblical indications of the age of the earth, apparently only several thousands of years old. Some of those scholars maintain that the 'day' referred to in the Creation story does not have the same meaning as is ordinarily associated with it, but rather must be literally defined as an indefinite period of time, perhaps even billions of years. For a good example of this kind of reasoning, see Bernard Ramm, *The Christian View of Science and Scriptures* (Grand Rapids: W. B. Eerdmans, 1954), p. 256.

A PRESCRIPTION

Much of the vast wisdom in the Bible can be unlocked, but only through genuine questioning, through the honest pursuit of truth. It is hoped that, as a result of having read this book, the reader can acknowledge that viewing the Bible as 'perfect' or 'inerrant' is a misguided approach to unlocking that wisdom. That acknowledgment need not limit one's respect for the Bible or one's ability to profit from its teachings. Intelligent questioning enables people to make the wisest possible use of the Bible. For, indeed, questioning any book, institution, or person need not be irreverent. It can be, in fact, an effective tool for improving one's understanding, and perhaps it is part of the antidote for the anguish that many current and former fundamentalists are now experiencing.

Appendix: FUNDAMENTALISTS ANONYMOUS

Fundamentalists Anonymous (F.A.) was founded in 1985 by Richard Yao, a Wall Street lawyer and graduate of Yale Divinity School, and James J. D. Luce, then a Wall Street banker. Within two years of its founding, membership had passed 30,000, and the organization has since continued to expand rapidly.

Yao has stated: "As soon as I was old enough, I was sent to a 'Christian' school run by the church. It was extremely authoritarian, rigid, and regimented. It was total immersion. I spent most of my waking hours either in the school or in the church. I was guilty, fearful, and anxious. I was very unhappy. They promised 'abundant life' but all I had was an endless nightmare. Gradually I decided I had to leave. But all my friends and most of my family were in the church. Covertly, I began to make friends outside the church. And when I left the fold, these friends became my informal support group. Years later, when I wondered why I made it and many of my friends didn't, I realized that this informal support system made all the difference for me. It gave me the courage to break out. And it sustained and helped me on the journey. Thus the idea for F.A."

F.A. is organized as a network of support groups for those who feel themselves to have been hurt or damaged by their experience of fundamentalism. F.A. has adopted the following 'Statement of Purpose', which is usually read at the start of each support group meeting:

> Fundamentalists Anonymous (F.A.) is a support organization for people who have been hurt by their fundamentalist experience [We use the term "fundamentalism" to include the charismatic/pentecostal movement]. We do not recruit members. F.A. is open to those who desire to break free of the fundamentalist mindset. Our membership includes former fundamentalists and adult children of fundamentalists.

Joining F.A. Family are the concerned parents, spouses, relatives and close friends of those who have been caught up in the fundamentalist movement.

F.A. is a secular (non-religious) organization. We are not anti-religious or atheistic, nor do we endorse any church or religion. We do not discuss theology, but address the fundamentalist mindset only. This mindset is a world view which sees everything in terms of black and white, and neither tolerates ambiguity nor allows questioning.

We exercise our right to speak out against any attempt to impose fundamentalist beliefs on the rest of society by coercion, intimidation, manipulation or legislation. We feel an obligation to make the public aware of our negative experience in fundamentalism and to warn those who are vulnerable to the fundamentalist mindset and world view.

Our goals are twofold: *first,* we join together to help free ourselves and others from the fundamentalist mindset; and *second,* we use our experiences to educate the public on the dangers of fundamentalism as a mental health hazard and on the fundamentalist movement as a serious threat to our way of life and our society's basic liberties.

F.A. has established a hotline (212-696-0240) and can be written to at P.O. Box 20324, Greeley Square Station, New York, NY 10001.

We have provided the above information, with the permission of Fundamentalists Anonymous, because we believe that it may be of assistance to some of our readers. The authors are not and never have been members of F.A., nor is F.A. responsible in any way for the writing or publishing of this book. The authors' views are not necessarily those of F.A., nor vice versa.

A further note of interest. The term 'fundamentalist' originated in Protestant Christianity but has spread to many other religions and cultures. The word 'fundamentalist' is now in use throughout the Islamic world. Professor Frederick M. Denny has informed us that in Muslim countries there has arisen great concern about the mental and emotional problems of those who have been made unhappy by their involvement in fundamentalist Muslim sects. As a result, in some Muslim countries, such as Indonesia and Bangladesh, there is strong interest in the American phenomenon of Fundamentalists Anonymous, and in the possibility of setting up similar support networks for distressed Muslim fundamentalists.

Finally, in the United States there has been formed a support network called Catholics Anonymous, for Roman Catholics. Details from: P.O. Box 5, Central Park Station, Buffalo, NY 14215.

WHAT TO READ NEXT

1. ABOUT THE BIBLE

A vast quantity of literature has been produced, especially in this century, concerning the historical influences upon the writing of the Bible and how the Bible came to be compiled. The extensive research and argument in this field is well-known to many Biblical scholars, but largely unknown to most people, including many active Christians.

The following list is in no way comprehensive. To the modern Biblical scholar, who must keep up with the latest developments, some of the information in these books is 'old hat'. The sole purpose of this bibliography is to give the lay person, fundamentalist or non-fundamentalist, a good starting-point for learning more about the Bible. (Naturally, we used far more than just these listed sources in our preparation for writing this book.)

Achtemeier, Paul J. *The Inspiration of Scripture: Problems and Proposals.* Philadelphia: Westminster Press, 1980.

Asimov, Isaac. *Asimov's Guide to the Bible: Old and New Testaments.* New York: Avenel Books, 1981. This easy-to-read book is a good place to start. It is aimed at illuminating the Bible by tying together a great deal of historical, geographical, and scientific information.

Barr, James. *Beyond Fundamentalism.* Philadelphia: Westminster Press, 1984. This book is somewhat more easy reading than the other three listed by Barr. Barr tries to develop a sound basis for an evangelical faith which is compatible with the acceptance of Biblical errancy. He discusses such topics as Biblical inspiration, the origins of the world, and Jesus and the Old Testament.

Barr, James. *The Bible in the Modern World*. New York: Harper and Row, 1973.

Barr, James. *Fundamentalism*. Philadelphia: Westminster Press, 1978.

Barr, James. *The Scope and Authority of the Bible*. Philadelphia: Westminster Press, 1981.

Beegle, Dewey M. *Scripture, Tradition, and Infallibility*. Grand Rapids: Eerdmans, 1973. This is a fairly easy-to-follow book aimed at showing that, while the Bible is accurate enough for the Christian faith, it bears the stamp of human limitations. As he examines revelation, canonicity, tradition, and authority, Dr. Beegle argues that inerrancy and infallibility are attributes only of God and Jesus, but not the Bible.

Bultmann, R. *Primitive Christianity in its Contemporary Setting*. New York: Meridian Books, 1956. An important work that has been influential among modern theologians, but it is not one of the easiest to grasp of those listed here. Bultmann tries to describe the intellectual and philosophical context in which early Christianity developed. The book reflects his desire to "interpret the movements of history as possible ways of understanding human existence."

Butterick, George A. *The Interpretor's Dictionary of the Bible* (four volumes). Nashville: Abingdon Press, 1962.

Eakin, Frank E., Jr. *Religion in Western Culture: Selected Issues*. Washington, D.C.: University Press of America, 1977.

Fosdick, Harry Emerson. *The Modern Use of the Bible*. New York: Macmillan, 1927. A well-written, historically sensitive introduction to some central ideas of the Bible. This book reflects many of the values and ideals of 'liberal Christianity'.

Gamble, Harry Y., Jr. 'Christianity: Scripture and Canon', in *The Holy Book in Comparative Perspective*, edited by Frederick M. Denny and Rodney L. Taylor. Columbia: University of South Carolina Press, 1985.

Gamble, Harry Y., Jr. *The New Testament Canon: Its Making and Meaning*. Philadelphia: Fortress Press, 1985.

Harvey, A. E. *The New English Bible Companion to the New Testament*. Cambridge: Cambridge University Press, 1970.

Hay, Malcolm. *Europe and the Jews*. Boston: Beacon Press, 1960. This book traces the history of anti-Semitism in Christendom, and explains how anti-Semitism was inspired by dubious readings of the New Testament. The author shows how some Biblical verses, especially in the Gospel of John, can be easily interpreted or misinterpreted to promote anti-Semitism.

Hoffman, R. Joseph. *Jesus Outside the Gospels*. Buffalo: Prometheus, 1984. A useful book containing virtually everything that is known about the historical figure of Jesus from early sources other than the Gospels.

Isaac, Jules. *The Teaching of Contempt*. Translated by Helen Weaver. New York: Holt, Rinehart and Winston, 1964.

James, Robison B. (editor) *The Unfettered Word*. Waco, Texas: Word Books, 1987. A fine discussion, by moderate Southern Baptists, of the problems with 'inerrancy'.

Keating, Karl. *Catholicism and Fundamentalism: The Attack on 'Romanism' by 'Bible Christians'*. Harrison, NY: Ignatius Press, 1988. We disagree with much of Keating's book, but it is well worth reading to appreciate the real strength of another point of view. The author is an outstanding Roman Catholic apologist, who in this book presents a very readable and hard-hitting defense of Catholic orthodoxy against Protestant fundamentalism. Keating criticizes the view that for Christians the Bible *alone* should be regarded as the source of Divine authority. Although opposed to *Protestant* fundamentalism, Keating is himself not free of fundamentalist assumptions.

Keck, Leander E. *Taking the Bible Seriously: An Invitation to Think Theologically*. New York: Association Press, 1962.

Klausner, Jacob. *The Messianic Idea in Israel.* New York: Macmillan, 1955.

Kraeling, Emil G. *The Clarified New Testament.* Vol. 1: *The Four Gospels.* New York: McGraw-Hill, 1962.

Marsden, George M. *Fundamentalism and American Culture.* New York: Oxford University Press, 1980.

Pagels, Elaine. *The Gnostic Gospels.* New York: Random House, 1979. Contrary to what most people imagine, first-century Christianity was far more varied and diverse in its range of beliefs and opinions than Christianity has ever been since. The New Testament represents the thinking of the one school or faction which became victorious and then suppressed the others. This is a beautifully clear exposition by a leading scholar of the ideas to be found in 'Gnostic' Christian writings as old as the New Testament, but very different in outlook.

Perrin, Norman, and Duling, Dennis C. *The New Testament: An Introduction.* New York: Harcourt, Brace, Jovanovich, 1982. Although well-written and designed for non-specialists, this book is fairly difficult in places. For most people, a book to be kept and referred to, rather than read straight through.

Rahtjen, Bruce D. *Biblical Truth and Modern Man.* Nashville: Abingdon Press, 1968.

Ringgren, Helmer. *The Messiah in the Old Testament.* Naperville, Ill.: Allenson, 1956.

Sheehan, Thomas. *The First Coming.* New York: Random House, 1986. This book summarizes for the non-expert what is known about the historical figure of Jesus, but its style is not popular. The reader may prefer to dip into it rather than read it through. Discusses the possibility that Jesus did not believe himself to be Divine, and did not intend to found a new religion.

Smith, Henry Preserved. *Inspiration and Inerrancy: A History and a Defense.* Cincinnati: Robert Clarke and Co., 1893. This book has left its mark. It reveals much about the nineteenth-century debate on the internal evidence of the inspiration and inerrancy of the Bible. Many of Smith's arguments compelled theologians to change the way they argued for inspiration and inerrancy.

Sunderland, J. T. *The Origin and Character of the Bible.* Boston: Beacon Press, 1922. A good introduction to some central ideas in the Bible, which is treated with respect but regarded as reflecting human limitations. Like the Fosdick work cited above, Sunderland's book is a good example of 'liberal Christian' thinking.

Teeple, Howard M. *The Historical Approach to the Bible.* Evanston: Religion and Ethics Institute, 1982. This book was written with the general reader in mind. It gives a good account of the methods historians use in studying the Bible.

Wells, G. A. *The Historical Evidence for Jesus.* Buffalo: Prometheus, 1982. An unusually skeptical, but calm and fair-minded, evaluation of the evidence for Jesus as a historical figure.

WHAT TO READ NEXT

2. CREATION AND EVOLUTION

We discussed creation and evolution briefly in Chapter 5. Many people are very ill-informed about what present-day biologists believe, so the following bibliography may be helpful.

Asimov, Isaac. *In the Beginning.* New York: Crown Publishers, 1981.

Beadle, George and Muriel. *The Language of Life: An Introduction to the Science of Genetics.* Garden City, NY: Doubleday, 1966.

Darwin, Charles. *The Origin of Species By Means of Natural Selection or The Preservation of Favoured Races in the Struggle for Life* [1859]. New York: New American Library, 1958.

Dawkins, Richard. *The Selfish Gene.* New York: Oxford University Press, 1976.

Dawkins, Richard. *The Blind Watchmaker.* New York: Norton, 1986. A defense of Darwin's theory of natural selection by a leading biologist. Dawkins concentrates on the question of whether complex organization (as in living organisms) could have come about without intelligent design.

Edwards, Fred (editor). *Creation/Evolution.* A journal produced by biologists and other scientists, devoted entirely to reporting Creationist claims and showing exactly why they are mistaken. Available from: P.O. Box 5, Amherst Branch, Buffalo, NY 14226.

Eldredge, Niles. *The Monkey Business: A Scientist Looks at Creationism*. New York: Washington Square Press, 1982. Unfortunately, this book has an unhelpful, sneering tone, guaranteed to repel those who don't already share the author's opinions. For readers who can stomach its provocative style, it is a clear, entertaining explanation of the reasons why most biologists reject Creationism. (Eldredge is one of those who disagree with the most widely-held account of *how* evolution has occurred, and are therefore often quoted by Creationists as proof that 'scientists are now rejecting evolution'!)

Gould, Stephen Jay. *Ever Since Darwin: Reflections in Natural History*. New York: Norton, 1977. The first of a series of very readable, popular accounts of developments in modern biology, especially the theory of evolution, made up of collected columns from *Natural History* magazine.

Gould, Stephen Jay. *The Panda's Thumb: More Reflections in Natural History*. New York: Norton, 1980.

Gould, Stephen Jay. *Hen's Teeth and Horse's Toes: Further Reflections in Natural History*. New York: Norton, 1983.

Greene, John C. *Darwin and the Modern World View*. New York: New American Library, 1963. A brief summary of Darwin's influence on modern thought, especially how the mainstream churches came to accept evolutionary theory.

Hoyle, F., and Wickramasinghe, N. C. *Evolution from Space: A Theory of Cosmic Creationism*. New York: Simon and Schuster, 1981. This book is by two scientists who moved from agnosticism to belief in God because of their finding that the evolution of life on Earth had to be directed by some outside intelligence. Very critical of Darwinism.

Kitcher, Philip. *Abusing Science: The Case Against Creationism*. Cambridge, Mass.: MIT Press, 1982.

Leakey, Richard. *The Making of Mankind*. New York: Dutton, 1977.

McGowan, Chris. *In The Beginning: A Scientist Shows Why the Creationists Are Wrong*. Buffalo: Prometheus, 1984.

Raup, David M. *The Nemesis Affair: A Story of the Death of Dinosaurs and the Ways of Science.* New York: Norton, 1986.

Ruse, Michael. *Darwinism Defended: A Guide to the Evolution Controversies.* Reading, Mass.: Addison-Wesley, 1982.

Sagan, Carl. *Cosmos.* New York: Random House, 1980.

Simpson, G. G. *The Major Features of Evolution.* New York: Columbia University Press, 1953.

Stanley, Steven M. *The New Evolutionary Timetable.* New York: Basic Books, 1981.

Strahler, Arthur. *Science and Earth History: The Evolution/Creation Controversy.* Buffalo: Prometheus, 1987.

Taylor, Gordon Rattray. *The Great Evolution Mystery.* New York: Harper and Row, 1983.

Williams, George C. *Adaptation and Natural Selection.* Princeton: Princeton University Press, 1966. An important and influential restatement of the theory of evolution. Not for the beginner.

Wysong, R. I. *The Creation-Evolution Controversy.* Midland, Mich.: Inquiry Press, 1976. This may be the best attempt to defend Biblical Creationism.

INDEX

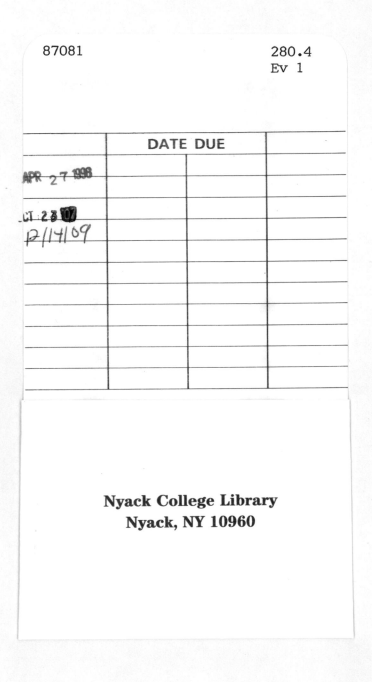